Christ Our Passover
Has Been Sacrificed

Christ Our Passover Has Been Sacrificed

A Guide through Paschal Mystery Spirituality Mystical Theology in *The Roman Missal*

Mark G. Boyer

WIPF & STOCK · Eugene, Oregon

CHRIST OUR PASSOVER HAS BEEN SACRIFICED
A Guide through Paschal Mystery Spirituality: Mystical Theology in *The Roman Missal*

Copyright © 2018 Mark G. Boyer. All rights reserved. Except for brief quotations in critical publications or reviews, no part of this book may be reproduced in any manner without prior written permission from the publisher. Write: Permissions, Wipf and Stock Publishers, 199 W. 8th Ave., Suite 3, Eugene, OR 97401.

Wipf & Stock
An Imprint of Wipf and Stock Publishers
199 W. 8th Ave., Suite 3
Eugene, OR 97401

www.wipfandstock.com

PAPERBACK ISBN: 978-1-5326-4221-0
HARDCOVER ISBN: 978-1-5326-4222-7
EBOOK ISBN: 978-1-5326-4223-4

Manufactured in the U.S.A. DECEMBER 1, 2017

Dedicated to
the musician who taught me
about dying and rising to new life:
Corbin S. Cole,
and the psychologist who taught me
about dying and rising to new life:
Matthew S. Ver Miller,
transparent universalizers,
full of divine love, grace, energy, and Spirit.

"It is truly right and just, our duty and our salvation, at all times to acclaim you, O Lord, but in this time above all to laud you yet more gloriously, when Christ our Passover has been sacrificed. For he is the true lamb who has taken away the sins of the world; by dying he has destroyed our death, and by rising, restored our life."

—Preface I of Easter

We are "always carrying in the body the death of Jesus, so that the life of Jesus may also be made visible in our bodies."

—2 Cor 4:10

"Very truly, I tell you, unless a grain of wheat falls to the earth and dies, it remains just a single grain; but if it dies, it bears much fruit."

—John 12:24

" . . . [T]he fundamental meaning of language lies in experience and is often indirect, and . . . we should keep the underlying experience in mind when we interpret religious discourse."

—James Feist

" . . . Christian spirituality . . . means being filled with the Holy Spirit, which finds expression in our daily self-giving to God and neighbors in imitation of Christ and in a Christian approach to everyday life. Liturgical theology points to the particular action of the Holy Spirit in the liturgy. Liturgical theology also addresses biblical spirituality, since the liturgy continuously places human beings before the face of God in Jesus Christ and confronts their lives with the transforming power of God's word. Within the sacramental re-presentation of the entire paschal mystery of Christ, this Word takes on a singular power as part of the very nature of the New Covenant. The task of the liturgy is therefore the ongoing transformation of human beings into Christ."

—Boguslaw Migut

"Wise people have always passed through a major death to their egocentricity. This is the core meaning of transformation."

—Richard Rohr

Contents

Abbreviations | xi
Notes on the Bible and The Roman Missal | xiii
Introduction | xvii

1. The Paschal Mystery | 1
2. Lent and Easter Seasons | 18
3. Palm Sunday | 23
4. Palm Sunday: Suffering is Betrayal for the Matthean Jesus | 28
5. Palm Sunday: Suffering is Abandonment for the Markan Jesus | 33
6. Palm Sunday: Suffering is Martyrdom for the Lukan Jesus | 41
7. Thursday of the Lord's Supper | 51
8. Friday of the Passion of the Lord: Part 1 | 58
9. Friday of the Passion of the Lord: Part 2 | 63
10. Friday of the Passion of the Lord: Part 3 | 70
11. The Easter Vigil in the Holy Night | 79
12. Easter Sunday of the Resurrection of the Lord | 86

Contents

13   The Ascension of the Lord | 93
14   Pentecost Sunday | 97
15   Anointing the Sick | 105
16   Death, Funeral, and Christian Burial | 110
17   Special Celebrations | 121

Conclusion | 131
Bibliography | 135
Recent Books by Mark G. Boyer | 139

Abbreviations

CHRISTIAN BIBLE (NEW TESTAMENT)

Acts = Acts of the Apostles
Col = Letter to the Colossians
1 Cor = First Letter of Paul to the Corinthians
2 Cor = Second Letter of Paul to the Corinthians
Gal = Letter of Paul to the Galatians
Heb = Letter to the Hebrews
Jas = Letter of James
John = John's Gospel
Luke = Luke's Gospel
Mark = Mark's Gospel
Matt = Matthew's Gospel
1 Pet = First Letter of Peter
Phil = Letter of Paul to the Philippians
Rev = Revelation
Rom = Letter of Paul to the Romans

HEBREW BIBLE (OLD TESTAMENT)

Exod = Exodus
Ezek = Ezekiel
Gen = Genesis
Isa = Isaiah
Joel = Joel
Josh = Joshua
2 Kgs = Second Book of Kings
Lev = Leviticus

Abbreviations

Mal = Malachi
Num = Numbers
Ps = Psalm
1 Sam = First Book of Samuel
2 Sam = Second Book of Samuel
Song = Song of Songs (Canticle of Solomon)

OLD TESTAMENT (APOCRYPHA)

Wis = Wisdom (of Solomon)

Notes on the Bible and *The Roman Missal*

THE BIBLE

THE BIBLE IS DIVIDED into two parts: The Hebrew Bible (Old Testament) and the Christian Bible (New Testament). The Hebrew Bible consists of thirty-nine named books accepted by Jews and Protestants as Holy Scripture. The Old Testament also contains those thirty-nine books plus seven to fifteen more named books or parts of books called the Apocrypha or the Deuterocanonical Books; the Old Testament is accepted by Catholics and several other Christian denominations as Holy Scripture. The Christian Bible, consisting of twenty-seven named books, is also called the New Testament; it is accepted by Christians as Holy Scripture. Thus, in this work:

- Hebrew Bible (Old Testament), abbreviated HB (OT), indicates that a book is found both in the Hebrew Bible and the Old Testament;
- Old Testament (Apocrypha), abbreviated OT (A), indicates that a book is found only in the Old Testament Apocrypha and not in the Hebrew Bible;
- and Christian Bible (New Testament), abbreviated CB (NT), indicates that a book is found only in the Christian Bible or New Testament.

In notating biblical texts, the first number refers to the chapter in the book, and the second number refers to the verse within the chapter. Thus, HB (OT) Isa 7:11 means that the quotation comes from Isaiah, chapter 7, verse 11. OT (A) Sirach 39:30 means that the quotation comes from Sirach, chapter 39, verse 30. CB (NT) Mark 6:2 means that the quotation comes from Mark's Gospel, chapter 6, verse 2. When more than one sentence appears in a verse, the letters a, b, c, etc. indicate the sentence being referenced in the verse. Thus, HB (OT) 2 Kgs 1:6a means that the quotation comes from the Second Book of Kings, chapter 1, verse 6, sentence 1.

In the HB (OT) and the OT (A), the reader often sees LORD (note all capital letters). Because God's name (Yahweh or YHWH, referred to as the Tetragrammaton) is not to be pronounced, the name Adonai (meaning *Lord*) is substituted for Yahweh when a biblical text is read. When a biblical text is translated and printed, LORD (cf. Gen 2:4) is used to alert the reader to what the text actually states: Yahweh. Furthermore, when the biblical author writes Lord Yahweh, printers present Lord GOD (note all capital letters for GOD; cf. Gen 15:2) to avoid the printed ambiguity of LORD LORD. When the reference is to Jesus, the word printed is Lord (note capital L and lower case letters; cf. Luke 11:1). When writing about a lord (note all lower case letters; cf. Matt 18:25) with servants, no capital L is used.

THE ROMAN MISSAL

The Roman Missal is the book of prayers used by a priest or bishop when celebrating the Eucharist, commonly referred to as saying Mass. In 1970, following the close of the Second Vatican Council, Pope Paul VI issued a new Roman Missal in Latin replacing the one issued by Pope Pius V in 1570 after the close of the Council of Trent. The Missal of Paul VI was emended in 1971 and issued in English in 1974. In 1975, a second edition in Latin was issued by Paul VI; it was issued in English in 1985. A third edition of *The Roman Missal* was issued in Latin by Pope John Paul II in 2002 and emended in 2008; however, it was not until 2011 that *The Roman Missal* was issued in English. Thus, all references made to *The Roman Missal* in this book refer to the 2011 English edition.

Here are some terms used in *The Roman Missal* with which the reader may not be familiar:

Celebration of the Eucharist = The Celebration of the Eucharist, commonly referred to as the Mass, consists of two parts: the Liturgy of the Word (two or three Scripture texts, a homily, the Creed, and General Intercessions) and the Liturgy of the Eucharist (a Eucharistic Prayer, the Our Father, and communion).

Collect = This is the opening prayer of the Eucharist (Mass) introduced by the priest or bishop with "Let us pray." It collects all the prayers of the congregants into one general, all-inclusive prayer.

Cycles A, B, and C = This designation refers to the three-year cycle of Scripture texts assigned to every Sunday of the liturgical year and found in the Lectionary, a five-volume set of books providing readings for Sundays,

Weekdays, and other sacramental celebrations. Cycle A (Matthew's Gospel) is used in 2020, 2023, 2026, etc. Cycle B (Mark's Gospel) is used in 2018, 2021, 2024, etc. And Cycle C (Luke's Gospel) is used in 2019, 2022, 2025, etc. During the weekdays of Lent and Easter, the biblical texts remain the same every year.

Easter Season = The Easter Season begins on Easter Sunday of the Resurrection of the Lord and lasts for fifty days. It ends with Pentecost Sunday. Easter Sunday is the first Sunday after the first full moon after the Spring or Vernal Equinox.

Eucharistic Prayer = This is the most important prayer of the Mass prayed by a priest or a bishop. During the narrative of all thirteen choices, the priest or bishop takes bread and remembers what Jesus did before he died—giving his body as bread—and takes a cup of wine and remembers what Jesus did before he died—giving his blood as wine. The prayer also includes a petition to God to send the Holy Spirit to make the bread and wine the body and blood of Christ as well as petitions for the pope, the local bishop, all the faithful, and the dead. It ends with a doxology to which all respond "Amen."

Lenten Season = The Season of Lent begins with Ash Wednesday, seven weeks before Easter. Lent ends on Holy Thursday evening, the Thursday before Easter Sunday.

Liturgical Year = The liturgical year begins with the First Sunday of Advent, usually the last Sunday of November or the first Sunday of December; The Advent Season lasts for four weeks. The Christmas Season begins on December 25, lasts three weeks, and ends with the Feast of the Baptism of the Lord, usually the second Sunday of January. The Lenten Season begins with Ash Wednesday, which can occur anytime in February or early March; it lasts six weeks and ends at the beginning of The Sacred Paschal Triduum with Thursday of the Lord's Supper, which can occur anytime from late March into early April. The Sacred Paschal Triduum ends on Easter Sunday evening. The Easter Season begins with Easter Sunday of the Resurrection of the Lord—usually falling in late March or early April—lasts fifty days, and ends with Pentecost Sunday, falling anytime between the middle of May and early June. In between the Christmas Season and the Lenten Season and in between the Easter Season and the next Advent is the Season of Ordinary Time—meaning counted weeks. The first section of Ordinary Time can be from two to ten weeks, and the second section of Ordinary Time can be from eleven to thirty-four weeks.

Mass = In *The Roman Missal*, Mass refers to the two parts of the Celebration of the Eucharist: the Liturgy of the Word and the Liturgy of the

Eucharist. The word *Mass*, from the Latin *missa*—from the Latin *mittere*, meaning *to send*—means to send away. The last line of the Mass in Latin is "Ite, missa est.," meaning "Go, the Mass is ended."

Prayer after Communion = This is a concluding prayer said by the priest or bishop after communion—the sharing of the body and blood of Christ—has finished.

Prayer over the Offerings = This is a prayer said by the priest or bishop after the gifts of bread and wine have been prepared, presented to God, and set on the altar.

Prayer over the People = This is a required prayer during Lent which follows the Prayer after Communion. While it may be used at other times, during Lent it asks God to bless people with his divine presence and help them during their journey through Lent to Easter.

Preface = This prayer, introduced with dialogue between the priest or bishop and the congregants, praises and thanks God for something specific, such as the resurrection of Christ. It begins the Eucharist Prayer and concludes with the Holy, Holy, Holy Lord acclamation. When several choices are provided, they are numbered, such as, Preface I of Easter, Preface II of Easter, etc.

All prayers of any kind in *The Roman Missal* are specified for every day of the liturgical year. Thus, in this book one may find a reference to Monday of the Third Week of Lent; this means that a set of prayers for the Eucharist on Monday of the Third Week of Lent is provided. A set consists of a Collect, a Prayer over the Offerings, a Prayer after Communion, and a Prayer over the People. Likewise, Thursday of the Fifth Week of Easter presents a Collect, a Prayer over the Offerings, and a Prayer after Communion. The prayers are addressed to God through Christ in the unity of the Holy Spirit.

Because *The Roman Missal* is a book of over 1,500 pages, it is subdivided by liturgical seasons (Advent, Christmas, Lent, Easter, and Ordinary Time), feasts, saints, ritual Masses, and more. Some subsections of *The Roman Missal* contain numbered paragraphs. Thus, when a reference appears in a footnote, it will often contain *par.*, the abbreviation for the word *paragraph*, or *pars.*, the abbreviation for the word *paragraphs*, when a range of numbered paragraphs are being referenced within a named subsection of *The Roman Missal*. Other subsections of *The Roman Missal* are not numbered. When this is the case, a page number is given in the footnote to the edition of *The Roman Missal* found in the bibliography of this book; this later case is indicated by only the page number.

Introduction

PRELUDE

NOT TOO LONG AGO a good friend and I were discussing the conjunction of several events in our lives. He had broken up with his girlfriend recently and gotten a job as a contemporary music director at a large church. I had given a retreat on a major theme of the Roman Catholic liturgy for Holy Thursday and Good Friday and, a few weeks later, watched the film *Collateral Beauty* (2016). Before all of that had taken place we had spent lots of time discussing the traces of death and new life in our lives beginning with the truth that relationships are grounded in vulnerabilities or weaknesses—death—and not in strengths—successes—as most people presume. Through our mutual relationship, and by reflecting on all the friendships we shared separately with others, we discovered how often we had died and risen to new life.

My friend's breaking the relationship with his girlfriend required some dying, which brought him transformation, and resulted in new life. Taking the job as a contemporary music director meant dying to lots of personal free time, being transformed by the ministry, and discovering lots of new life through music, relationships with band members, congregants, and leadership members. In order to accept the job he had to die willingly to weekend trips home and some family ties to church. The dying and new life that occurred in me was the result of letting go of control and learning to trust the person with whom I shared a relationship; he challenged me to reveal my true self to him, to transform my strict schedule into a flexible one, and to remove my fear of losing him through his presence in my life. While both of us were actively engaged in dying and new life, both of us had read some of Martin Buber's thought, and both of us had listened to a sermon which brought the theme of dying and rising to our consciousness again. Buber would have been proud of our dialogical approach!

In the midst of all this conjunction I began to realize that genuine, pure love requires death in order for new life to flow. We don't like hearing about dying because we live in a death-denying culture that cannot begin to wrap its head around the end of physical life as we know it. Instead of dying, people pass away or just pass. But there is more to dying than final death, but final death seems to be a blockade that keeps us from the wisdom of real living. If we take the time to examine it, we begin to notice that dying and new birth, transformation, occur all the time in our lives. "Life is tied to death in love. . . . "[1] McCosker refers to this as "living death, or better dying-kind-of-life."[2] Getting in contact with the process might be called relinquishing, turning loose, or submitting. I prefer the negative-connoting, paradoxical, oxymoronic wisdom contained in the understanding that human spiritual transformation occurs when we have died and discovered new life. However, if the final-death blockade is in place, then the wisdom of dying and new life can never be grasped.

Religious and spiritual readers will, of course, immediately jump to applying my words to Jesus of Nazareth, who was crucified, died, was buried, and raised from the dead. However, that limits the spiritual wisdom of the universal theme that permeates all of life by applying it to only one person. From the moment we are born we are dying and rising. From the moment we are born we are relinquishing, turning loose, and submitting. If we don't rebel against the process—but most of us do!—then not only do we get good at living, but we also get very good at dying! Deep in our flesh we learn the truth that transformation through death to new life is

1. McCosker, "*Enhypostasia Mystica*," 83.
2. Ibid.

required for those who want to be fully alive. Those of us who write about the spiritual life refer to this as human wholeness. And human wholeness encompasses spiritual wholeness as well. What this means is that we do not truly live until we have embraced our finitude, our end, our death.

Wholeness—human and spiritual—is a lifetime process of getting better and better at dying and rising.[3] In other words, wholeness is a lifetime process of transformation. It is recognizing that genuine love requires dying. Genuine love between two people sparks transformation that requires both of them to die in order to rise to new life. This is not a one-time only event; it continues as long as the relationship endures—and maybe even beyond! Likewise, the genuine love shared in the transformation process of dying and rising is nothing other than grace, energy, or divinity. God is always in the process of transformation; that is what God revealed in Jesus through his death and resurrection. Our human relationships are simultaneously divine relationships. (Again, Buber would be proud!) And as such, the love within them requires death and results in new life. God is present, revealing his presence and working through our human relationships. God is present revealing the very mystery of the Trinity through dying and rising. The life of the three persons of the Trinity is an eternal process of transformation through submission or dying in order to share new life. And we, through our love relationships, are invited to participate in it in order to experience the wholeness of God.

If this understanding at first seems culturally contradictory, it is. We live in a culture that places all its emphasis on power, clinging to stuff, and accumulating wealth because in the popular way of thinking those guarantee life. The simple truth of the matter is that they do not. Nothing can guarantee real life, not even life insurance! Real life—fleshy and spiritual—is all about getting good at transformation, getting good at dying and rising. And once we experience the truth of transformation, well, then we begin to realize how death and resurrection are genes on our DNA helix. The non-patriotic freedom that results from the realization enables us to embrace the dying and rising process because transformation leaves us overwhelmed with grace, energy, and divinity. And that is the wisdom that all world religions in their unadulterated and non-politicized forms attempt to teach us.

My friend has learned this truth by reflecting on the events of his life. A broken shoulder from a football tackle caused lots of dying to playing

---

3. Boyer, *Human Wholeness*.

the sport, but it also resulted in lots of new life on the other side of healing. The transformation that occurred was full of grace. Leaving home for college was a dying experience, but it resulted in the life of new friends, new avenues of learning, new ideas, and lots of energy through learning. The transformation made him realize not only how smart he was, but also how wise he was. Accepting a job requiring that he clock in at 3:30 a.m. required dying to some evening activities in order to accept the new life that a steady income from work offered. The transformation meant getting to bed early so as to be able to arise early. His whole day had to be reorganized.

The love relationship with my friend required dying in my life. It required the letting go of my role as mentor and his as mentee. To my surprise I discovered that I could be mentored if I stopped offering solutions and listed to the wisdom sitting in front of me. My usual 5:30 p.m. dinner was moved to 7:30 or 8 p.m. because of his schedule. At first I found myself rebelling against the change, but I wanted to keep the relationship. Flexibility became a new word in my vocabulary. Dying to my scheduled life brought about a transformation to new, energized, and divine life. I became aware of other limitations that I was putting on what a relationship had to be; these, too, had to be let go so that I could behold the real beauty of the other. Now, instead of offering solutions, I prefer a mutual investigation of an observation.

These are but a few examples of dying and rising—there are many more. As both of us were experiencing them and reflecting upon them weekly, we became aware of how the transformation process had always been present in our lives. That awareness enabled us to delve more deeply in understanding dying and rising as spirituality, and it also challenged us to articulate it with the goal of understanding it better ourselves and teaching it to others. If, indeed, we have discovered this great truth, then some others have also discovered it. We know how we have struggled to articulate it, and we hope that putting that struggle into words will help others come to know the wisdom of dying and rising and embrace the transformation that overflows with life.

THIS BOOK

In Roman Catholicism, we hear the phrase *paschal mystery* used often in liturgies (Baptism, Eucharist, Anointing the Sick, Funerals, during the Seasons of Lent and Easter, and in some feast day celebrations) throughout the year. For most people, that is all it is: a two-word phrase. We don't know what it means if we even recognize that we have heard it. So, we ignore it or pass over it. It may get our momentary attention because it occurs often during Lent and even more often during the Easter Season, but it is of little or no concern to us to research it or delve into what it might mean.

This book examines the paschal mystery. The phrase, probably coined by St. Augustine in the fifth century CE, is used it to describe the death and resurrection of Jesus. The full understanding of the phrase will be explored in depth below. Suffice it now to say that the phrase needs to be applied to us. What happened to Jesus is happening to us today. We must make the connection to the theme that Augustine recognized in the life of Jesus of Nazareth. Otherwise, all of liturgy is merely remembering. After understanding exactly what paschal mystery is, then we need to make it our own. By celebrating what happened to Jesus, we are celebrating what is happening to us. In other words, the death and resurrection of Jesus is a universal theme that is traced in our lives. The work before us, therefore, is not just understanding how it was lived by Jesus, but understanding how we live it today.

One of the greatest themes in Christian spirituality, both biblical and liturgical, is the meaning of the death and resurrection of Jesus. The biblical accounts do not use the phrase *paschal mystery*, but they do attempt to interpret and apply the events of the death and resurrection of Jesus to the people living at the end of the first century and the beginning of the second century CE. Liturgical texts, specifically Roman Catholic ones, do use the phrase *paschal mystery*. Those texts, updated periodically in terms of translation, attempt to interpret and apply the events of the death and resurrection of Jesus to the people living today at the beginning of the twenty-first century CE. While there is plenty of connection between the first-century and twenty-first century biblical and liturgical texts, most of the conjunction is lost on modern people who are not engaged in the scholarly work of mining the links. Paschal mystery represents a rich seam of spiritual truth which will not only be presented in the pages that follow, but will also be reflected upon in the hope of helping the reader apply this truth to his or her life. Paschal mystery spirituality reminds us that heaven is now; eternal life is now; the kingdom preached by Jesus is experienced now through dying and rising.

Introduction

TITLE

The title of this book, *Christ Our Passover Has Been Sacrificed*, is taken from the Easter Prefaces in *The Roman Missal*.[4] In the preface, which begins the Eucharistic Prayer of Mass, the priest or bishop declares that it is truly right to acclaim God and loud him yet more gloriously during the fifty days of the Easter Season when Christ our Passover has been sacrificed. The Easter Season begins with the Easter Vigil during the night before Easter Sunday and concludes with Pentecost Sunday fifty days later.

The word *Christ* in the title/phrase refers to the risen Jesus. In Greek, the word for *anointed* is *christ*; in Hebrew, the word for *anointed* is *messiah*. Claiming that Jesus is the Christ, the anointed one, indicates that he, like others before him, was called and commissioned by God for a specific purpose. According to *The Roman Missal*, Jesus was anointed with the Spirit.[5] Christ does not indicate divinity, although that is often associated with the title. For example, the priest/prophet/judge Samuel is sent by God to David to anoint him as king of Israel and Judah. After Saul's death, David is anointed again (1 Sam 16:1–13; 2 Sam 5:1–5). The prophet Isaiah refers to Cyrus, King of Persia, as God's anointed (Isa 45:1) and specifies his purpose as such (Isa 44:28; 45:13). To be an anointed one is to be called, commissioned, and entrusted with a divine mission. Thus, the word *christ* refers to Jesus, God's anointed one, who was raised from the dead. His resurrection confirms his status as an anointed one.

The phrase *our passover* applies the meaning of the Hebrew Bible (Old Testament) Passover to Jesus. While more will be said about this below, suffice it to say at this point that the multi-event Passover narrated in the Hebrew Bible (Old Testament) Book of Exodus results in people facing death and emerging alive. For example, the death of a lamb, whose blood was applied to the doorposts and lintel of Hebrew homes, preserved the lives of those inside while the firstborn of Egyptians perished (Exod 12:1–51). Jesus was crucified, died, and was raised from the dead. Thus, he like his forbearers faced imminent death—indeed, he died—and came out alive. In other words, he passed over through death to life. Thus, he is the new passover.

Jesus was sacrificed. That is what his crucifixion is all about. The phrase is part of a sentence from Paul's First Letter to the Corinthians. The apostle

---

4. *Roman Missal*, "Order of Mass," pars. 45–50.
5. Ibid., "Thursday of Holy Week [Holy Thursday]: The Chrism Mass," pars. 7, 12.

writes, "... Our paschal lamb, Christ, has been sacrificed" (1 Cor 5:7b). Paul explicitly makes the connection between the Passover lamb described in the Book of Exodus and Jesus. Just as the Passover lamb was slaughtered at twilight so its blood could be placed on the doorposts and lintels of the Hebrews' homes in order to insure their lives (Exod 12:6–7), so was Jesus slaughtered on the cross and raised from death to life (that is, he passed over) to insure the lives of believers.

SUBTITLES

The first subtitle of this book is *A Guide through Paschal Mystery Spirituality*. The paschal mystery, a phrase used repeatedly in Roman Catholic liturgies, collectively refers to the suffering, death, resurrection, ascension, and gift of the Spirit of Jesus. The phrase compacts into one the major events of the life of Jesus, who was recognized as the Christ through resurrection from the dead. According to Regan, before Vatican Council II, the phrase *paschal mystery* was seldom, if ever, employed.[6] He notes that before *The Roman Missal* of Pope Paul VI, issued in 1969, the phrase was used in only two prayers, in which it referred to the eucharistic sacrifice of the Mass.[7] With the publication of Paul VI's *Missal*, however, the phrase appears throughout the 1500-page book. More will be said about this below.

The word *spirituality* attempts to capture "the heart of what it means to be in relationship with God."[8] According to White, "The Christian spiritual path has at its center the opening up of our hearts to the Spirit of God, so that rooted in the Divine mystery, we may fall more and more in love with the source of life."[9] Of course, liturgy of any kind plays a central role in spirituality, especially paschal mystery spirituality, because it brings us into "the transforming presence of an all-embracing God."[10] Simply put, paschal mystery spirituality is participating in the suffering, death, resurrection, ascension, and gift of the Spirit of Jesus. It is a practical spirituality, a lived spirituality, a cooperative spirituality between God and the individual person in relationship to all humanity. An in-depth exploration of paschal mystery spirituality is presented below.

6. Regan, "Centrality of the Paschal Mystery," 129.
7. Ibid.
8. White, "Liturgical Spirituality," 244.
9. Ibid.
10. Ibid., 245.

Introduction

This book serves as a guide through paschal mystery spirituality. If the reader considers this a journey, then I serve as the guide through liturgical texts in *The Roman Missal* and through biblical passages which give rise to paschal mystery spirituality.

The second subtitle for this book is *Mystical Theology in The Roman Missal*. Mystical theology is systematic reflection on the experience of a loving knowledge of God.[11] The experience of God is mediated through the prayers in *The Roman Missal*. In other words, "God's hidden and mysterious work of grace within a community and a person's life"[12] are interpreted through the prayers found in *The Roman Missal*, particularly those dealing with Jesus' suffering, death, resurrection, ascension, and gift of the Spirit. In a word, we are exploring paschal mystery spirituality in an attempt to appropriate the prayers of *The Roman Missal* and the biblical texts upon which the prayers are based.

If we appropriate the prayers and the biblical texts upon which they are often based, we are awakened to our own mystical experiences of the past and/or prepared for them in our future. Mystical experiences connect us and keep connecting us in deeper and deeper levels, helping us to realize that God is "all in all" (1 Cor 15:28). Mystical experiences are divine experiences of universal connections through all people to intimacy, partnership, and cooperation with God.

I will guide the reader to knowledge about paschal mystery spirituality and, through reflection upon it, help him or her to connect life experiences to it. In other words, the reader has experienced God when celebrating Eucharist, especially during the Lenten Season and the Easter Season, and by bringing together the prayers from *The Roman Missal* and biblical texts, he or she integrates the experiences of God by reflection on the experiences. My goal is "to make intelligible one's orientation to God as it is experienced and often known only implicitly in the guise of ordinary daily living" and ecclesial celebrations.[13] God, in the person of Jesus Christ, drives the human to awareness of paschal mystery spirituality in his or her life and calls forth responsible living of it in ever-transformative relationships.

---

11. Welch, "Mystical Theology," 692.
12. McKim, *Westminster Dictionary*, 181.
13. Welch, "Mystical Theology," 693–4.

Introduction

ORGANIZATION OF THIS BOOK

Because this book attempts to connect paschal mystery spirituality to the life of the reader, it dialogues with *The Roman Missal* and the Bible. We begin with an in-depth definition of the paschal mystery in order to be sure we know exactly what the phrase means. Following that we examine its use during the liturgical seasons of Lent and Easter. These seasons are calculated according to the phases of the moon. Easter is always the first Sunday after the first full moon following the Spring (Vernal) Equinox, which occurs between March 19 and March 21. Thus, Easter Sunday can occur anytime between March 19 and April 25! Once Easter is calculated, then we count back six Sundays to arrive at the First Sunday of Lent, and the Wednesday before that is Ash Wednesday, the beginning of Lent. Counting forward from Easter Sunday, we find Pentecost, the fiftieth day of Easter or the eighth Sunday of Easter.

The last week of Lent is called Holy Week. It is during Holy Week that the paschal mystery shines. Thus, chapters in this book are devoted to Palm Sunday of the Passion of the Lord and each of the three gospels that are read on a three-year rotation basis on this Sunday. The last days of Holy Week—Thursday, Friday, Saturday—are referred to as the Sacred Paschal Triduum. Each day focuses on a different aspect of the paschal mystery, although all aspects are present. Thus, chapters in this book are devoted to Thursday of the Lord's Supper, Friday of the Passion of the Lord, and the Easter Vigil in the Holy Night and Easter Sunday. According to the Acts of the Apostles, forty days after Easter Sunday is the Ascension of the Lord. Thus, a chapter explains this aspect of paschal mystery spirituality. Because Pentecost Sunday ends the Easter Season, a chapter is also devoted to that day.

Even though the paschal mystery is particularly present during Lent and Easter, it, nevertheless, permeates other liturgical celebrations as well. Thus, chapters are presented on Anointing the Sick; Death, Funeral, and Christian Burial; and Special Celebrations.

Because knowledge about something is incomplete unless it is connected to the lives of people, each chapter contains a reflection which attempts to bridge the gap between knowledge about the paschal mystery and how it is already being lived or how it might be lived by people today—paschal mystery spirituality. In other words, what happened to Jesus is happening or should be happening to those who follow him. Following the reflection the reader will find a series of questions which are designed to make personal and communal connections to the specific aspects of the

Introduction

paschal mystery presented in the chapter. By dialoguing with the questions, paschal mystery spirituality can be nourished. I recommend that the answers to the questions be recorded in a journal, not just for reference purposes, but to note one's growth in paschal mystery spirituality.

It is my ardent hope and prayer that the reader of this book will not only learn about the aspects of the paschal mystery of Jesus, but that he or she will also see the traces of the paschal mystery in his or her life and choose to deepen them or see them in a new light. The goal of all spirituality is personal transformation that flows from the individual out into the community. It begins with our awareness that we are already one with God. By listening to another—in this case reading my words—the seeds for further transformation are planted. As they take root and begin to sprout, the reader delves ever deeper into paschal mystery spirituality and is able to articulate how what happened to Jesus is happening in the life of his follower.

Mark G. Boyer

1

The Paschal Mystery

BASICALLY, THE PASCHAL MYSTERY refers to the suffering, death, resurrection, ascension, and gift of the Spirit of Jesus. According to the "Universal Norms on the Liturgical Year and the Calendar" in *The Roman Missal*, " . . . Christ accomplished his work of human redemption and of the perfect glorification of God principally through his paschal mystery, in which by dying he has destroyed our death, and by rising restored our life. . . . "[1] Thus, in its basic form, the paschal mystery "comprises the passion and resurrection of Christ."[2] However, besides the passion (suffering and death) and resurrection, the other aspects of ascension and gift of the Spirit are also found in the ninety-day Lent and Easter seasons of the liturgical year.

Indeed, paschal mystery is mentioned throughout *The Roman Missal*—usually with capital letters, that is, Paschal Mystery. Most of the references to paschal mystery occur in prayers said during the forty-day Season of Lent, the Sacred Paschal Triduum (Holy Thursday, Good Friday, the Easter Vigil, and Easter Sunday), and the fifty-day Season of Easter. According

---

1. *Roman Missal*, "Universal Norms," par. 18.
2. Regan, "Centrality of the Paschal Mystery," 136.

to Regan, this serves "to impart unity and direction to the entire period from Ash Wednesday to Pentecost."[3] Phiri says that "[t]he celebration of the paschal mystery . . . is synonymous with the celebration of the gospel as God's great promise in which we participate for our own transformation and that of others into a life of beatitude."[4]

COLLECTIVE USE

Thus, the paschal mystery is often used in a collective sense. The five major events of the saving actions of Jesus mentioned above are collected as one and named the paschal mystery. Lent, which begins with Ash Wednesday, prepares people to celebrate the paschal mystery, according to the first prayer for the blessing of ashes.[5] Likewise, the Preface for the First Sunday of Lent mentions worthily celebrating the paschal mystery;[6] the Collect for Thursday of the Third Week of Lent asks God to help people to press towards the worthy celebration of the paschal mystery;[7] and the Collect for Tuesday of the Fourth Week of Lent requests that people worthily welcome the paschal mystery.[8]

In the opening remarks for Palm Sunday of the Passion of the Lord, the priest or bishop explains that the local congregation is gathered with the whole church to begin the celebration of the Lord's paschal mystery; he explains this by referring to his passion (suffering and death) and resurrection.[9] Likewise, one of the Prayers for the beginning of the Friday of the Passion of the Lord [Good Friday] service states that by shedding his blood Jesus established the paschal mystery.[10]

The most extensive use of the paschal mystery is found during the Easter Vigil. Its first mention is in the prayer after the second reading.[11] In the second optional prayer after the seventh reading, God is reminded that

3. Ibid., 126.
4. Phiri, "Liturgical Participation," 227.
5. *Roman Missal*, 210.
6. Ibid., 218.
7. Ibid., 243.
8. Ibid., 251.
9. Ibid., "Palm Sunday of the Passion of the Lord," par. 5.
10. Ibid., "Friday of the Passion of the Lord [Good Friday]," par. 6.
11. Ibid., "Easter Sunday of the Resurrection of the Lord: The Easter Vigil in the Holy Night," par. 25.

he instructs and prepares people to celebrate the paschal mystery.[12] And in the address to the congregants before they renew their baptismal promises, the priest or bishop reminds everyone that it is through the paschal mystery that they have been buried with Christ in baptism so that they may walk with him in newness of life.[13]

God gave the paschal mystery, according to the Collect for Friday within the Octave of Easter.[14] According to the Collect for Saturday of the Second Week of Easter, God has cancelled the sentence written by the law of sin through the paschal mystery.[15] God is constantly accomplishing the paschal mystery according to the Collect for the Fifth Sunday of Easter.[16] The Collect for Saturday of the Sixth Week of Easter asks God to shape minds with the practice of good works and help people strive to hold fast to the paschal mystery.[17] Pentecost Sunday makes it very clear that the paschal mystery consists of the fifty days of the Easter Season. The Collect for the Vigil Mass refers to this as does the Preface.[18]

Other references to the paschal mystery occur in Preface I of the Sundays in Ordinary Time,[19] Preface VI of the Sundays in Ordinary Time,[20] and in the Collect of the Votive Mass of The Most Holy Eucharist.[21]

Indirectly, the paschal mystery is referred to as the drawing-ever-closer feast of salvation,[22] the solemn celebrations to come,[23] the coming festivities,[24] the present festivities,[25] and the celebration of Easter.[26] Those

---

12. Ibid., par. 30.
13. Ibid., par. 55.
14. Ibid., 393.
15. Ibid., 402.
16. Ibid., 418.
17. Ibid., 437.
18. Ibid., 451, 456.
19. Ibid., "Order of Mass," par. 52.
20. Ibid., "Order of Mass," par. 57.
21. Ibid., 1333.
22. Ibid., 243.
23. Ibid., 246.
24. Ibid., 255.
25. Ibid., 391.
26. Ibid., 417.

who have been redeemed by Jesus' passion (suffering and death) rejoice in his resurrection.[27]

PLURAL USE

Sometimes the plural form, paschal mysteries, is used to indicate the five major events of the saving actions of Jesus. For example, the Collect for Saturday of the Third Week of Lent mentions that hearts are set on the paschal mysteries,[28] as does the Prayer over the People for Wednesday of Holy Week.[29] During the Easter Season, the use of paschal mysteries is even more pronounced. Paschal mysteries is mentioned once during the Easter Vigil[30] and once at the Mass on Easter Sunday.[31] People find delight in the paschal mysteries;[32] through the paschal mysteries the gates of God's mercy are opened;[33] celebrating the paschal mysteries is God's gift;[34] and people pray to be conformed to the paschal mysteries.[35]

OTHER USES

There are a minimum of twelve other uses of the word *paschal*. First, in Preface I of Lent, God is reminded that during Lent people await the sacred paschal feasts, while the Solemn Blessing given during the Easter Vigil refers to Easter as the paschal feast and the collect for the Second Sunday of Easter refers to the yearly recurrence of the paschal feast.[36] Second, the Prayer over the Offerings for the Second Sunday of Lent asks God to

---

27. Ibid., 410, 416.
28. Ibid., 245.
29. Ibid., 289.
30. Ibid., "Easter Sunday of the Resurrection of the Lord: The Easter Vigil in the Holy Night," par. 61.
31. Ibid., "Easter Sunday of the Resurrection of the Lord: At the Mass during the Day," par. 76.
32. Ibid., 394, 398, 407, 411, 413, 421, 427.
33. Ibid., 402.
34. Ibid., 412.
35. Ibid., 423.
36. Ibid., "Order of Mass," par 39; "Easter Sunday of the Resurrection of the Lord: The Easter Vigil in the Holy Night," par. 68; 395.

sanctify people for the coming celebration of the paschal festivities,[37] while the Collect for Thursday of the Fourth Week of Lent asks God to bring his servants safely to the paschal festivities.[38] The Prayer over the People for Monday of Holy Week asks for God's protection so that his people may celebrate the paschal festivities with both bodily and mindful observance.[39] The Collect for Saturday of the Seventh Week of Easter refers to the fact that for seven weeks people have celebrated paschal festivities.[40]

Third, during the Easter Vigil while blessing the fire, the priest or bishop mentions the paschal celebrations,[41] and, fourth, before beginning the Liturgy of the Word, the priest or bishop exhorts the congregants to pray that God may complete his paschal work.[42] Fifth, one of the petitions of Lent II mentions the coming paschal solemnity.[43] Sixth, the Collect for Friday of the First Week of Lent asks God to conform the pray-ers to the paschal observances,[44] and the Collect for Monday of the Sixth Week of Easter also refers to the paschal observances.[45]

The seventh reference using the word *paschal* is paschal sacrifice.[46] Closely aligned with paschal sacrifice is the eighth reference: paschal banquet;[47] the ninth reference: paschal sacrament;[48] and the tenth reference: paschal offerings.[49] In the Collect for Tuesday within the Octave of Easter, God is praised for bestowing the paschal remedies, the eleventh reference using the word *paschal*,[50] as well as in several other places. Finally,

---

37. Ibid., 226.
38. Ibid., 253.
39. Ibid., 287.
40. Ibid., 444.
41. Ibid., "Easter Sunday of the Resurrection of the Lord: The Easter Vigil in the Holy Night," par. 10.
42. Ibid., "Easter Sunday of the Resurrection of the Lord: The Easter Vigil in the Holy Night," par. 22.
43. Ibid., 1467.
44. Ibid., 224.
45. Ibid., 426.
46. Ibid., 400; "Eucharistic Prayer for Use in Masses for Various Needs I, II, III, IV," par. 7.
47. Ibid., "Thursday of Holy Week [Holy Thursday]: The Chrism Mass," par. 12.
48. Ibid., "Easter Sunday of the Resurrection of the Lord: The Easter Vigil in the Holy Night," par. 67; 389, 396, 400, 405, 415, 419, 425, 434, 1375.
49. Ibid., 393.
50. Ibid., 390, 397, 405.

the twelfth reference is to paschal joy. This last phrase is found in all of the Prefaces for Easter and Ascension,[51] as well as in the Prayer over the Offerings during the Mass on Easter Sunday in which it is called paschal gladness.[52]

THE *PASCHAL* OF PASCHAL MYSTERY

With the understanding that paschal mystery in many different phrases permeates *The Roman Missal,* now a fuller explanation stemming from the Bible—both the Hebrew Bible (Old Testament) and the Christian Bible (New Testament)—needs to be grasped. It is best explained by beginning with a reflection on its basis in the Hebrew Bible (Old Testament) and, then, an exploration as to how it is applied to the life of Jesus.

The word *paschal* is synonymous with *passover*, a word used several times in *The Roman Missal* in addition to the references given in the description of the title of this book.[53] Pasch or Passover can refer either to Easter or Passover. Likewise, the adjective *paschal* can be used to describe either Easter or Passover. The Israelite Passover is the annual celebration of the exodus of the Hebrews from Egypt. The main course for the Passover meal was a lamb, which recalled the lamb's blood sprinkled on the doorposts of the Hebrews' houses. Seeing the blood, the Lord passed over these houses and spared the first born from death.

The genesis of the Passover is found in the book of Exodus:

> The LORD said to Moses and Aaron in the land of Egypt, " . . . Tell the whole community of Israel: . . . Every one of your families must procure for itself a lamb, one apiece for each household. . . . With the whole assembly of Israel present, it shall be slaughtered during the evening twilight. They shall take some of its blood and apply it to the two doorposts and the lintel of every house in which they partake of the lamb. . . . It is the Passover of the LORD. For on this same night I will go through Egypt, striking down every first-born of the land, both man and beast. . . . But the blood will mark the houses where you are. Seeing the blood, I will pass over you; thus,

---

51. Ibid., "The Order of Mass," pars. 45–51; 1469.

52. Ibid., "Easter Sunday of the Resurrection of the Lord: At the Mass during the Day," par. 73.

53. Ibid., "Appendix to the Order of Mass: Eucharistic Prayer for Reconciliation I," pars. 3, 7; "Palm Sunday of the Passion of the Lord," par. 18.

when I strike the land of Egypt, no destructive blow will come upon you." (Exod 12:1, 3, 6–7, 11–13)

Later, in the same chapter, the book of Exodus records how Moses promulgated the Passover. The author writes:

> Moses called all the elders of Israel and said to them, "Go and procure lambs for your families, and slaughter them as Passover victims. Then take a bunch of hyssop, and dipping it in the blood that is in the basin, sprinkle the lintel and the two doorposts with this blood. For the LORD will go by, striking down the Egyptians. Seeing the blood on the lintel and the two doorposts, the LORD will pass over that door and not let the destroyer come into your houses to strike you down." (Exod 12:21–23)

The first Passover, then, is God's literal passing over of the Hebrews' homes, which have been smeared with the blood of the Passover lamb. Later, this lamb is referred to as the paschal lamb. Not only does God pass over, but the Hebrews pass over. They pass over from imminent death to life. They pass over from slavery to freedom. The blood of the lamb saves them.

More passovers follow this one. Once the Hebrews march out of Egypt, they are led by a "column of cloud by day" and a "column of fire by night" (Exod 13:22). They arrive on the shore of the Red Sea, where Pharaoh and his army catch up with them. However, the Book of Exodus records: "The angel of God who was going before the Israelite army moved and went behind them; and the pillar of cloud moved from in front of them and took its place behind them. It came between the army of Egypt and the army of Israel" (Exod 14:19–20a). The "angel of God" is another way to refer to the presence of God. Not only does God lead the Israelites from slavery to freedom, God also protects them by moving between them and their enemies. In other words, God passes over his people again to save them. Throughout both the Hebrew Bible (Old Testament) and the Christian Bible (New Testament), the pillar of cloud and fire become signs of God's protective presence of people; they are also two of the elements of a theophany.[54]

The next Passover follows the movement of the cloud. " . . . Moses stretched out his hand over the sea. The LORD drove the sea back by a strong east wind all night, and turned the sea into dry land; and the waters were divided. The Israelites went into the sea on dry ground, the waters

---

54. Boyer, *Divine Presence*, 34–41, 64–73.

forming a wall for them on their right and on their left" (Exod 14:21–22). In other words, the Israelites pass over from imminent death—at the approach of Pharaoh and his military force—to life. God saves them again.

Joshua, Moses successor as leader of the Israelites, is modeled after the great prophet in the Hebrew Bible (Old Testament) Book of Joshua. This is seen very clearly in the account of Joshua leading the Israelites through the Jordan River, which is, of course, modeled after Moses leading them through the Red Sea. When the feet of the priests bearing the ark of the LORD dip into the edge of the Jordan River "the waters flowing from above stood still, rising up in a single heap far off. . . . Then the people crossed over. . . . When all Israel were crossing over on dry ground, the priests who bore the ark of the covenant of the LORD stood on dry ground in the middle of the Jordan, until the entire nation finished crossing over the Jordan" (Josh 3:16–17). Thus, like Moses, Joshua leads the Israelites through imminent death to new life into the land God promised to Abraham.

In the Second Book of Kings in the Hebrew Bible (Old Testament), the prophet Elijah is also modeled after Moses. So, before a chariot of fire and horses of fire descend from heaven so Elijah can ascend in a whirlwind into heaven (2 Kgs 2:11), Elijah "took his mantel and rolled it up, and struck the water; the water [of the Jordan River] was parted to the one side and to the other" and he and his successor, Elisha, "crossed on dry ground" (2 Kgs 2:8). Thus, Elijah not only passes over from this life to the next, but before that he passes over the Jordan River just like Moses and the Israelites had done many years before.

Elisha, modeled after Elijah, immediately picks up Elijah's mantle, which fell from him while he ascended. This is the same mantle Elijah had used to call Elisha (2 Kgs 19:20). "He took the mantel of Elijah that had fallen from him, and struck the water. . . . When he had struck the water [of the Jordan River], the water was parted to the one side and to the other, and Elisha went over" (2 Kgs 2:14). Thus, Elisha passes over the Jordan River.

The institution of the Passover and these other Passover events are the background to understanding the unique reference to Jesus as "the lamb of God" by the author of John's Gospel. Hermeneutically, the author of John's Gospel interprets Jesus' death and resurrection—his paschal mystery—in light of the Passover lamb. According to the Fourth Gospel, when John the Baptist sees Jesus coming toward him, he says, "Here is the Lamb of God who takes away the sin of the world!" (John 1:29) Later, John the Baptist watches Jesus walk by and says to two of his disciples, "Look, here is the

Lamb of God!" (John 1:36) The author makes his reference clear after Jesus' death, when he records, " . . . The soldiers came and broke the legs of the first and of the other who had been crucified with [Jesus]. But when they came to Jesus and saw that he was already dead, they did not break his legs. Instead, one of the soldiers pierced his side with a spear, and at once blood and water came out. . . . These things occurred so that the scripture might be fulfilled, 'None of his bones shall be broken'" (John 19:32–34, 36). As will be seen below, these last words describe the preparation of the lamb in the Book of Exodus (12:46).

In John's Gospel, Jesus does not eat a Passover meal with his disciples as he does in the Synoptic Gospels (Mark, Matthew, Luke). In John's Gospel he washes their feet during a meal on the (Thursday) evening before the Passover. The author makes this clear when his captors take Jesus to Pilate. He records, " . . . [T]hey took Jesus from Caiaphas to Pilate's headquarters. It was early in the [Friday] morning. They themselves did not enter the headquarters, so as to avoid ritual defilement and to be able to eat the Passover" (John 18:28). After Pilate declares that he finds no guilt in Jesus, he reminds them, " . . . You have a custom that I release someone to you at the Passover" (John 18:39).

Because Pilate cannot satisfy the crowd, he relents and condemns Jesus to death by crucifixion. Before the sentence is handed down, the author states: "[I]t was the day of Preparation for the Passover; and it was about noon" (John 19:14a). Noon, the time that Jesus was condemned to death, was also the time that the priests in the temple would have begun slaughtering the paschal lambs. Thus, Jesus is portrayed as being condemned, crucified, and dying at the same time as the paschal lambs are being slaughtered in the temple in preparation for the Passover. That is why John's Gospel declares him to be the Lamb of God.

The author goes to extremes to be sure that the reader understands his connection between the Hebrew Bible (Old Testament) Passover lamb and the new passover lamb—Jesus. Immediately after Jesus dies, he writes: "Since it was the day of Preparation, the Jews did not want the bodies left on the cross during the sabbath, especially because that sabbath was a day of great solemnity. So they asked Pilate to have the legs of the crucified men broken and the bodies removed" (John 19:31). In other words, according to John's Gospel, in the year that Jesus died, Passover fell on the sabbath (Saturday); this means that preparation for it had to be completed before sunset on Friday. After Jesus is buried in a tomb in a garden, the author also tells the reader, "... Because it was the Jewish day of Preparation, and the tomb was nearby, they laid Jesus there" (John 19:42). Jesus had to be buried before sunset so that those who buried him could celebrate the Passover.

The quotation, "None of his bones shall be broken" (John 19:36), which is fulfilled by the soldier's action of not breaking Jesus' legs, is the author's reference to the regulations concerning the preparation of the Passover lamb. The book of Exodus records that the Lord told Moses, "... [Y]ou shall not break any of its bones" (Exod 12:46; Num 9:12). By the time the reader gets to this point in John's Gospel, there can be no doubt that the author understands Jesus, the Lamb of God, to be the replacement for the lamb slaughtered in the temple before Passover began at sunset.

Also, the reader should note the liturgical hermeneutic at work. Keeping in mind the title of this book, *Christ our Passover Has Been Sacrificed*,[55] Jesus' death is his self-sacrifice from which he passed over to resurrected life. To further emphasize this hermeneutic, Preface V of Easter states that by the oblation of his body, Christ brought to fulfillment the previous sacrifices on the cross. By doing so, he showed himself to be the priest, the altar, and the lamb of sacrifice.[56] The Easter Proclamation (Exsultet), a long hymn sung only once a year during the Easter Vigil, reflects upon how Christ paid Adam's debt to the Father by pouring out his own blood. Then, the hymn declares that these are the feasts of passover, in which is slain the lamb, the one true lamb, whose blood anoints the doorposts of believers. This night commemorates the Hebrews' passing dry-shod through the Red Sea, the night that the pillar of fire banished the darkness, when Christ broke death and rose victorious from the dead.[57] Thus, the hermeneutical move is complete. The blood of Jesus saves people like the blood of the lamb once put into motion the events that saved the Hebrews. This is why the author of John's Gospel refers to Jesus as the Lamb of God. This is why *The Roman Missal* refers to Christ as the Paschal Lamb[58] who has entered the eternal Pasch.[59] Preface I of Easter states that Christ is the true lamb who has taken away the sins of the world. Through his dying, he has destroyed

---

55. *Roman Missal*, "Easter Sunday of the Resurrection of the Lord: The Easter Vigil in the Holy Night," pars. 24, 66, 75.

56. Ibid., "Order of Mass," par. 49.

57. Ibid., "Easter Sunday of the Resurrection of the Lord: The Easter Vigil in the Holy Night," par. 19.

58. Ibid., 1136.

59. Ibid., 1212.

death, and through his rising to new life, he has restored life.[60] Preface III of Easter declares him to be the sacrificial victim, the lamb once slain who lives forever.[61] And Preface V of Easter calls him the lamb of sacrifice.[62]

The author of John's Gospel uniquely portrays one solider opening up the side of Christ (John 19:34), much like God opens up the side of Adam in the Book of Genesis (2:21–22), and blood and water flow out. The blood of the new passover lamb not only saves people from their sins, as John the Baptist had made clear in the beginning of John's Gospel (1:29), but it becomes the cup from which they drink when they remember his death in the supper they celebrate in his memory. Instead of sprinkling the blood of bulls on the people, as Moses did (Exod 24:8), now people drink his blood under the appearance of wine. A new people is born from the side of Christ. They are initiated into this new corporate body through the water of baptism, as had been explained to Nicodemus earlier in John's Gospel (3:1–21).

In John's Gospel, then, Jesus is portrayed as the new passover or paschal lamb. He is slaughtered on the cross. However, he is saved. God raises him from the dead. Jesus passes over from death to life. The Christian Bible (New Testament) Book of Revelation attempts to capture this truth by presenting "a Lamb standing as if it had been slaughtered" (Rev. 5:6). Every person who is initiated as a follower of Jesus through water also passes over from eternal death to eternal life. Just as the lamb was used as a yearly remembrance of the Hebrews' and Israelites' Passover from death to life, so the wine of Eucharist and the water of baptism are used by the Christian to remember Jesus' Passover from death to life and the Christian's initiation into this great event—the paschal mystery.

The Passover of Elijah mentioned above becomes the background to understanding the transfiguration of Jesus in the Synoptic Gospels (Mark, Matthew, Luke). Not only does Elijah appear with Jesus on a mountain—the typical place for a theophany[63]—but Moses, the man upon whom Elijah is modeled, also appears with him. The earthly Jesus is transfigured into the resurrected Christ. There is little doubt that that the author of Mark's Gospel created this event (Mark 9:2–8) to serve as his resurrection account, since there is no sighting of the resurrected Christ at the original ending

---

60. Ibid., "Order of Mass," par. 45.
61. Ibid., par. 47.
62. Ibid., par. 49.
63. Boyer, *Divine Presence*, 1–9.

of Mark's Gospel (16:8). Furthermore, the Markan Jesus instruction to his three disciples specifically references death and resurrection (Mark 9:9–10).

Following his Markan source, the author of Matthew's Gospel presents the story of the transfiguration, but uses it as a foreshadowing of things to come (Matt 17:1–8). As in Mark, the Matthean Jesus instructs his three disciples not to tell about the vision until he has been raised from the dead (Matt 17:9).

The author of Luke's Gospel also follows his Markan source for the transfiguration narrative. However, he understands it to proclaim the paschal mystery, without, of course, using that phrase. Unique to Luke's narrative (Luke 9:28–36) is the note that Moses and Elijah discuss Jesus departure, which he was to accomplish in Jerusalem (Luke 9:31). The word translated *departure* is *exodus* in Greek!

Elijah's translation into heaven in a chariot of fire and horses of fire—light—are found in the Christian Bible (New Testament) descriptions of Jesus' face shining like the sun and his dazzling white clothes—light—(Mark 9:3; Matt 17:2, Luke 9:29). Just as Elijah passed over from earthly life to new or heavenly life by ascending in a whirlwind into heaven (2 Kgs 2:11), so Jesus passed over through death to new life. The accounts of Jesus' transfiguration attempt to interpret the meaning of resurrection: life is changed, not ended.[64] The author of Luke's Gospel further likens Jesus to Elijah by portraying Jesus ascending into heaven (Luke 24:51; Acts 1:9).

THE *MYSTERY* OF PASCHAL MYSTERY

The second word of the phrase *paschal mystery* now needs to be understood. Mystery does not refer to that which cannot be comprehended. The word *mystery* means hidden, as God is not available to our senses. Some physical sign mediates the divine presence.[65] It is helpful to think of mystery as invisible spiritual substance[66] or the core of a person's being.[67] Mystery is the energy that surges within us, the electricity that runs through our DNA wiring. It is an interior form of religious experience.[68] Commonly referred to as spirituality, it is the divine spark that kindles a fire under us

---

64. Ibid., "Order of Mass," par. 78.
65. Boyer, *Divine Presence*, 83–88.
66. Kramer, *Martin Buber's Spirituality*, xxii.
67. Ibid., xxxv.
68. Zachhuber, "Mysticism," 72.

and prompts us to act; according to the Collect for the Second Sunday of Lent, it is spiritual sight made pure.[69] It is the living experience of God. So that the spark is not extinguished it needs tending; once it is fully aglow it starts fires in others. Thus, mystery is best defined as the means which God chooses to reveal God's self, his very being, often referred to as grace, to people. In other words, God revealed himself through the Passover events in the past; those events are theophanies, manifestations of the divine presence, a type of divine self-revelation.[70] God continues to make God's presence know in events today. And, in the future, God will reveal that God is saving and protecting his people.

In the sprinkling of the blood of the Passover lamb, in the fire, in the passing over of the cloud, and in the crossing of the Red Sea, God was revealing himself. God revealed himself in Joshua's, Elijah's, and Elisha's crossing the Jordan River. Likewise, in the suffering, death, resurrection, ascension, and gift of the Spirit of Jesus, God was revealing himself. Jesus permitted God to shine through his fragile, suffering humanity. By dying, Jesus brought an end to death. By rising, he revealed new life on the other side of the grave. God triumphed through Jesus' suffering. God promises all that he will do the same for them. In other words, God demonstrates his faithfulness in the person of his anointed, Jesus. And as will be seen, the same faithfulness is demonstrated in all those who are baptized and anointed. Thus, just as God was at work in the death and resurrection of Jesus, so God is at work in the death and resurrection of those who have been initiated as followers of Jesus. People find God in the same death and new life where Jesus found God. Thus, mystery is the felt relationship one has with the divine and the world. Feelings lead to actions, and actions are classified as experiences one has in solitude with the divine. Sometimes mystery is called a state of conscious awareness or of the presence of the divine in the dailyness called life. Some people refer to mystery as an experience of intimacy with the divine or an immediate perception of the presence of God.

The Roman Missal refers to mystery as being caught in the fire of the Spirit[71] or the fire of divine love.[72] It is how God wipes away all that is old in

---

69. *Roman Missal*, 226.
70. Boyer, *Divine Presence*, xiii.
71. *Roman Missal*, 233.
72. Ibid., 237–8.

people, increases grace in them, and brings about newness of life.[73] In other words, one lives a holy way of life,[74] passing over from old life to new life.[75] Mystery is accomplished through God's cleansing of people from old ways and transforming them into new creations.[76]

The Roman Missal repeatedly refers to spirituality as making people partakers of the one supreme Godhead.[77] This occurs through the exchange of bread and wine into the body and blood of Christ. Because people become what they eat and drink, when they eat the body of Christ and drink his blood, they become the body and blood of Christ. And since Christ is the second person of the Trinity, they partake of the one Godhead. Such knowledge should lead people to a worthy way of life—which is paschal mystery spirituality.

Morgan adds a further and deeper dimension to this concept. He writes that "when God acts, [people] act with God; [people] act insofar as God acts through [them]. . . ."[78] Likewise, people "become what [they] love."[79] Thus, "by loving God [they] can therefore become God."[80]

REFLECTION

Because there is no time with God, it is true to say that God is always in the process of making God's presence known in the world. Thus, every daily event has the potential to be an event which reveals God's protective love for people and saves them. The practice of paschal mystery spirituality ultimately leads to human wholeness, a spiritual union with the divine. This union is both the movement of God toward the person and the responsive movement of the person toward God. Spiritual wholeness means that one is wholeheartedly present to the suffering, death, resurrection, ascension, and gift of the Spirit. In other words, a person is united with Jesus. The union or wholeness is never complete because the process lasts a lifetime. It is a way of life, an ongoing seamless integration of body, mind, heart, and spirit.

73. Ibid., 252.
74. Ibid., 254.
75. Ibid., 254, 260.
76. Ibid., 391.
77. Ibid., 398, 408, 414, 418, 422, 428.
78. Morgan, "How to Read a Mystical Text," 96.
79. Ibid., 97.
80. Ibid.

The Paschal Mystery

As an in-process person always moving toward wholeness, one encounters God and others (world, community) which spark further wholeness. There is a direction in paschal mystery spirituality which becomes the way one lives in spirit with God and others. In other words, the force of one's being is propelling forward.

Jesus is the model for paschal mystery spirituality. According to Loades, " . . . [T]he historic Christ was the first human person to exhibit in all [his] completeness the spiritual possibilities of human beings, followed by all those in whom a comparable life-process and growth takes place, representing 'a true variation of the human species'. . . . "[81] He changes the human mind about God, who desires to grace people with a relationship. In Jesus God spills blood to get to people, then he raises the deceased to new life. Spirituality, which concerns the things affecting the human spirit, involves a relationship with the divine spirit, who permeates everything alive. Thus, paschal mystery spirituality is a way of living in realization that God shares in life's suffering, death, resurrection, ascension, and spirit; God renews the world through mysteries beyond all telling.[82] The spiritually aware person sees that all life is holy, that passion leads to the glory of the resurrection,[83] that people are redeemed by Jesus' passion so they can rejoice in the resurrection.[84]

Furthermore, this transparency to the divine has a ripple effect, that is, it affects others. A person's personal paschal mystery spirituality moves out of ego to a deeper sense of living in relationship to everything else alive in the world and, thus, to God, In other words, paschal mystery spirituality refers "to an inter-human dialogical grace that transforms one from self-centered, self-obsessed individuality to a life of ever-new, ever-genuine relationships between [one] and the world, [one] and God."[85] The process of paschal mystery—suffering, death, resurrection, ascension, and spiriting—continues to repeat itself always going deeper and deeper.

Jesus is a model of the authentic human being; he entered into a unique, unreserved relationship with God. He became a partner with God, trusting him all the way through his life to his death. Because of his faithfulness, God raised him from the dead as a model for others. His ascension

---

81. Loades, "Mysticism," 125.
82. *Roman Missal*, 250.
83. Ibid., 227–8.
84. Ibid., 393, 401, 418, 436.
85. Kramer, *Martin Buber's Spirituality*, 137.

gives a new vision to his followers. And his gift of the Spirit connects to every human spirit who desires the intimate relationship. This is why his paschal mystery has to become our paschal mystery. We need to transform our negative view of suffering into a positive appreciation for the change it begins to produce in us. We need to learn how to die instead of spending all our energy on preserving life. Abundant trust of God results in new life,[86] a new vision of who we are, and a new inspiriting.

Paschal mystery spirituality is transformative; it is a way of living that encompasses primarily daily dying and rising. The other elements of suffering, ascension, and spirit are also present, albeit often subtly. Suffering leads to dying. Dying leads to new life. Resurrection leads to a new vision, and a new perspective is permeated by spirit and Spirit. We learn how to live this way with models: Abraham, Moses, Elijah, Ezekiel, Jesus, Paul, Matthew, Mark, Luke, John.

This is for what we pray. On the Fifth Sunday of Easter, we ask God to constantly accomplish within us the paschal mystery.[87] On Friday of the Fifth Week of Easter, we seek to be rightly conformed to the paschal mysteries.[88] While it is not mentioned in the Prayer after Communion on Good Friday, it is clearly indicated by the declaration that we are restored to life by the death and resurrection of Christ.[89] On the Feast of Sts. Philip and James, May 3, we ask for a share in the passion and resurrection of Christ;[90] on the Optional Memorial of St. Rita of Cascia, May 22, we pray that we may more deeply participate in Jesus' paschal mystery;[91] and on the Memorial of Our Lady of Sorrows, September 15, we ask to participate in the passion and resurrection of Jesus just like his mother did so that we might complete in ourselves what is lacking in Jesus' sufferings (Col 1:24).[92]

1. How would you explain the paschal mystery to a friend?
2. In what specific ways have you experienced the paschal mystery in church, prayer, homilies, etc.?

---

86. *Roman Missal*, 257–8.
87. Ibid., 418.
88. Ibid., 423.
89. Ibid., "Friday of the Passion of the Lord [Good Friday]," par. 30.
90. Ibid., 858.
91. Ibid., 864.
92. Ibid., 949.

3. How have you experienced the paschal mystery in your life? Which of the five aspects—suffering, death, resurrection, ascension, gift of the Spirit—has been most prominent? How?

4. Watch the film *Collateral Beauty* (2016). Notice the three main points: death, time, and love. Considering *Collateral Beauty* is presenting paschal mystery spirituality as it is lived in the lives of the main characters in the film with divine prompting from angels, what is its primary paschal mystery focus?

5. Regan states that "Lent prepares for [the paschal mystery], starting already on Ash Wednesday, and Easter Time extends it over fifty days, enriching it with the ascent of Jesus and descent of the Spirit."[93] How have you experienced Regan's insight in your observance of the liturgical year, especially Lent and Easter?

6. When you ask God to constantly accomplish within you the paschal mystery, to participate and share in it, and to be conformed to it in order to complete what is lacking in Jesus' sufferings, what are the consequences? In other words, how have you been transformed by paschal mystery spirituality?

---

93. Regan, "Centrality of the Paschal Mystery," 138.

2

Lent and Easter Seasons

LENTEN SEASON

According to the "Universal Norms on the Liturgical Year and the General Roman Calendar," "Lent . . . prepares for [the] celebration of the paschal mystery both catechumens, by the various stages of christian initiation, and the faithful, who recall their own baptism. . . ."[1] The "Universal Norms" statement echoes "The Constitution on the Sacred Liturgy" from Vatican Council II: "The two elements which are especially characteristic of Lent—the recalling of baptism or the preparation for it . . . should be given greater emphasis in the liturgy. . . ."[2] Lenten preparation culminates in the Easter Vigil with the baptism of the elect; baptism plunges them into the paschal mystery. On the night celebrating the passover of Jesus, the church also celebrates the suffering, death, and resurrection of those who are willing to enter the watery tomb and emerge from the womb reborn and filled with the Spirit. Throughout Lent, catechumens prepare for their initiation during the Easter Vigil. Those who have already been baptized remember

1. *Roman Missal*, "Universal Norms," par. 27.
2. "Constitution," par. 109.

their baptism, prepare to celebrate the paschal mystery, and renew their baptismal promises at the Easter Vigil and on Easter Sunday.[3]

Lent begins with Ash Wednesday forty-six days before Easter Sunday in the liturgical calendar. The day is called Ash Wednesday because ashes, the remains of the previous year's palm branches, are traced on the foreheads of people in the form of a cross. One of the two formularies which may be used by the priest, bishop, deacon, or designated lay person states: "Remember that you are dust, and to dust you shall return."[4] The words come from God's curse of the man in the Hebrew Bible (Old Testament) Book of Genesis (3:19). While on the surface the words seem disconnected from the paschal mystery, in fact they identify one aspect of it: death. Every single person will die some day, and every single person spends a lot of time and energy avoiding this paschal mystery truth! Lent begins with an invitation to face one's mortality which, simultaneously, links Jesus' mortality to each person through the sign of the cross. Jesus' death on the cross calms the fear of death with the promise of resurrected life.

Yes, smearing living people's foreheads with dead ashes in the form of a cross is paradoxical. It looks contradictory, but it speaks a deeply hidden truth about the need to die in order to experience new life. It reminds people that reality is filled with contradictions; disciplined suffering is one way to reconcile life and death. It turns those who participate in paschal mystery spirituality into agents of transformation even as they are being transformed.

The Season of Lent is a call for discipline. Throughout this penitential season, the Christian is challenged to evaluate his or her life and to make whatever changes in it that he or she deems necessary for a fuller living of the gospel; this is often referred to as penance. Notice that people begin with baptism and evaluate how well they are living it. God gives them the strength to purify their hearts and to be freed from disordered affections. God also teaches them how to live in this passing world and hold onto the world that will never end.[5] Some might call this conversion, but the purpose of Lent is to focus on some change which needs to be made in one's life, to make it, and to begin to live it. Thus, at the end of Lent a transformation will have taken place; people will be living their baptism to a greater degree.

3. *Roman Missal*, "Universal Norms," par. 27.
4. Ibid., 211.
5. Ibid., "Order of Mass," par. 40.

Disciplined suffering is needed. Lent is the opportunity to begin a change that will last a lifetime. Thus, popular disciplines often include going on a diet, enrolling in a quit-smoking program, joining a health club, etc. Dieting, quitting smoking, and working out call for disciplined suffering. During Lent people can begin such a change in their lives, so that they can continue to live their new life throughout the rest of the liturgical year. Lent, then, becomes a miniature of one aspect—discipline—which always should be present in one's life. Those who live a disciplined life discover that they are transformed through disciplined suffering, just as Jesus was transfigured through suffering and death. Lenten transformation begins with baptism and involves an evaluation of how one's life conforms to the paschal mystery. A change, which involves disciplined suffering, in one's life is made and lived during Lent.

SACRED PASCHAL TRIDUUM

In between Lent and Easter, the church marks the Sacred Paschal Triduum. The word *sacred* means *holy*; the word *paschal* means *passover*; and the word *triduum* means *three*. The last three days of Holy Week, beginning with Holy Thursday evening, flowing through Good Friday (one day), continuing through Holy Saturday (two days), ends with Easter Sunday evening (three days). This is why the "Universal Norms" declare that "the Sacred Paschal Triduum of the passion and resurrection of the Lord shines forth as the high point of the entire liturgical year."[6] The "Constitution" explains that Jesus achieved the task entrusted to him by God "principally by the paschal mystery of his blessed passion, resurrection from the dead, and glorious ascension. . . ."[7]

Regan explains that the "Constitution" placed "the passion and resurrection of Christ within the larger category of the paschal mystery."[8] Thus, the Sacred Paschal Triduum of the passion and resurrection of the Lord, beginning with the evening Mass of the Lord's Supper on Holy Thursday and including Good Friday of the Passion of the Lord, has its center in the Easter Vigil and closes with Evening Prayer on the Sunday of the Resurrection.[9] In other words, the Triduum "celebrates the paschal mystery,

---

6. Ibid., "Universal Norms," par. 18.
7. "Constitution," par. 5.
8. Regan, "Centrality of the Paschal Mystery," 131.
9. *Roman Missal*, "Universal Norms," pars. 19–20.

understood to be both the life-giving passion of the Lord as well as his resurrection, that it extends through Easter Sunday, but that it begins only on Thursday evening with the Mass of the Lord's Supper."[10] Thus, according to Regan, "both aspects of the one paschal mystery are now included in the liturgies of all three days."[11] The Paschal Triduum is mentioned here in order to note its high point within the liturgical year. Each of its days is developed below with an emphasis on the paschal mystery.

EASTER SEASON

"The fifty days from the Sunday of the Resurrection to Pentecost Sunday are celebrated in joy and exultation as one feast day, indeed as one 'great Sunday,'" according to the "Universal Norms."[12] During the Easter Season, the baptized celebrate the new life which results from the changes which they made in their lives during Lent. Through disciplined suffering, they die to their old ways of living and rise to a new way of life. The Easter Season, then, is not a time to give up on what was accomplished during Lent, but, rather, a period to re-affirm commitment to change, to live the changes more deeply, and to insure that they will remain forever.

The gospel for the Second Sunday of Easter is the same in all three cycles. The Johannine account of Jesus' appearance on Easter Sunday evening, his bestowal of the gift of the Spirit, and the narrative about Thomas being absent that evening but present one week later and coming to faith is proclaimed (John 20:19–31). In John's Gospel, Pentecost occurs on Easter Sunday evening, not fifty days later as it does in the Acts of the Apostles. The same gospel will be proclaimed at the end of the Easter Season on Pentecost Sunday. This fact is mentioned here in order to show the unity of paschal mystery spirituality throughout the Easter Season.

REFLECTION

If, indeed, the Season of Lent is a call for discipline and a challenged to evaluate our lives in order to make changes that enable us to live a fuller baptismal life of dying and rising, then the Sacred Paschal Triduum presents

---

10. Regan, "Centrality of the Paschal Mystery," 131.
11. Ibid., 132.
12. *Roman Missal*, "Universal Norms," par. 22.

the opportunity for us to unite the paschal mystery that has been occurring in us with that of Jesus. In other words, if our focus during Lent has been a reflection on our baptism and changing our lives in order to conform to its dying and rising, then the three days between Lent and Easter not only acknowledge the transformation that has been taking place in us, but they interpret it in light of the transformation that occurred in the life of Jesus, called the paschal mystery.

The fifty days of the Easter Season become "one feast day"[13] celebrating the new life which results from the changes which we made in our lives during Lent. By reflecting on our baptism and engaging in disciplined suffering, we died to our old ways of living and rose to a new way of life. Then we united the paschal mystery traced in our life through baptism to that of Jesus' paschal mystery celebrated through the Sacred Paschal Triduum. The Easter Season, then, becomes not a time to give up on what we accomplished during Lent, but, rather, a period to re-affirm our commitment to change, to live the changes more deeply, and to insure that they will remain with us forever. The transfiguration that has occurred in us has taken root. Now, we recognize that the paschal mystery of Jesus is the same paschal mystery spirituality that we live every day.

1. How do you live your baptism? How does your observation of Lent help you evaluate your lifestyle in light of your baptism?

2. What is the connection between baptism and paschal mystery spirituality? In what specific experiences of your life do you find the connection?

3. How does paschal mystery spirituality permeate your life, especially during Lent, the Sacred Paschal Triduum, and the Easter Season?

4. In what specific ways have you applied a disciplined suffering to your life (during Lent)?

5. How has the past Sacred Paschal Triduum been a celebration of both Jesus' and your paschal mystery: suffering, death, resurrection, ascension, and gift of the Spirit?

6. How has the past Easter Season been a celebration of your new life resulting from your Lenten observance?

7. Why is Lent not a time to give up something—like candy, TV, or pizza—only to return to it later on Easter?

13. Ibid.

3

Palm Sunday

TECHNICALLY NOT PART OF the Sacred Paschal Triduum, Palm Sunday of the Passion of the Lord is the beginning of Holy Week and presents the first reference to the paschal mystery during the most solemn week of the liturgical year. The introduction to the day explains that the church recalls the entrance of Jesus into Jerusalem to accomplish his paschal mystery.[1] The priest or bishop introduces the liturgy by reminding all that the reason they have assembled is to celebrate the beginning of the paschal mystery, the death and resurrection of Jesus.[2]

The reading from the prophet Isaiah from the Third Song of the Servant of Yahweh (Isa 50:4–7) introduces the suffering aspect of paschal mystery. The passage contains the strophe which indicates the willingness of the servant to submit to insults and beatings. A grave insult is permitting one's beard to be plucked. The suffering servant states: "I gave my back to those who struck me, and my cheeks to those who pulled out the beard;

---

1. *Roman Missal*, "Palm Sunday of the Passion of the Lord," par. 1.
2. Ibid., par. 5.

I did not hide my face from insult and spitting" (Isa 50:6). The liturgical hermeneutic presents some of Jesus' suffering (passion) predicted in Isaiah.

Parts of Psalm 22 are used as a response to this reading. The refrain, "My God, my God, why have you forsaken me?" is taken from verse 1 of the same psalm and echoes the last words of Jesus in Mark's Gospel (15:34) and Matthew's Gospel (Matt 27:46). One particular verse focuses on suffering: "My hands and feet have shriveled; I can count all my bones" (Ps 22:16b–17a). Again, the words of the psalm are projected as an interpretation of Jesus' suffering (passion).

The suffering theme is continued in the reading from Paul's letter to the Philippians. The hymn, quoted in this letter, is used by Paul to exemplify the attitude which the Philippians should have toward suffering. Paul tells them to have among themselves the same attitude of Jesus, "who though he was in the form of God, did not regard equality with God as something to be exploited, but he emptied himself, taking the form of a slave, being born in human likeness. And being found in human form, he humbled himself and became obedient to the point of death—even death on a cross" (Phil 2:6–8). The same section of the hymn is quoted in the verse sung before the gospel. Thus, all Scripture texts before the actual proclamation of the gospel text narrating the suffering and death of Jesus have set the hermeneutical stage for understanding the passion, suffering, and death of Jesus paradoxically. The hymn makes clear that Jesus won by losing! His descent is his ascent! Thus, if Jesus' journey is one of self-emptying in order to be filled by God, then those who follow Jesus have to be transformed through suffering into new life just as he was. In other words, to die is to become—this is the pattern of paschal mystery spiritual transformation. God is not found by adding more life, but, paradoxically, God is discovered through the process of dying. God finds people who are dying and raises them to new life, just like he found the dying Jesus and transformed his cross into resurrected life.

For most people this requires a daily death to self, a letting go, an emptying. One's true self is who one is before God. One's true self is not who a person thinks himself or herself to be. That false self must die. Only when no one (false self) is left is a person aware that his or her true self is bigger than death, yet born of death.[3] Death is essential to the transition to life. Rohr writes:

3. Rohr, "Our Ultimate Identity."

> No one oversees his or her own demise willingly, even when it is the false self that is dying. God has to undo our illusions secretly, as it were, when we are not watching and not in perfect control, say the mystics. We move forward in ways that we do not even understand and through the quiet workings of time and grace. . . . Spirit initiates deep resonance and intimacy with our spirit, as the Endless Divine Yes evokes an ever-deeper yes in us. . . . The mystic is one who says, "Look what love has done to me. There's nothing left but God's intimate love giving itself to me as me."[4]

In other words, one must become like an empty vessel before God, who fills the person (vessel) with his own life, ever-new, ever-grace, ever-spirit. God transforms death into life.

On Palm Sunday of the Passion of the Lord, the emphasis is not primarily on the blessing and procession with palm branches—a sign of victory—but on the passion—suffering and death—of Jesus. The gospel for this day is introduced as the passion of the Lord Jesus Christ. Regan insists that the procession with palm branches forms a theological link to the reading of the passion through the paschal mystery.[5] He says that the commemoration of the Lord's entrance into Jerusalem is presented as "being already his entrance upon the passion, the passion that culminates in resurrection."[6]

Since *The Lectionary* employs a three-year cycle of readings, only every third year is the same account of the passion of Jesus read on Palm Sunday of the Passion of the Lord. Matthew's version, referred to as Cycle A, is read in 2020, 2023, 2026, etc. Mark's version, Cycle B, is read in 2018, 2021, 2024, etc. Luke's version, Cycle C, is read in 2019, 2022, 2025, etc. Each of the gospel accounts of the passion emphasizes different themes. They are explored in separate chapters below.

The suffering aspect of the paschal mystery is found in the Collect of the Mass. Jesus is presented as an example of humility; he took flesh and submitted to the cross.[7] On behalf of the congregation the priest or bishop prays that the assembly will learn his lesson of patient suffering.[8] The Prayer over the Offerings mentions the Lord's passion, that is, his suffering and

---

4. Ibid., "Dark Night."
5. Regan, "Centrality of the Paschal Mystery," 134.
6. Ibid.
7. *Roman Missal*, "Palm Sunday of the Passion of the Lord," par. 20
8. Ibid.

death.⁹ The Preface also mentions his suffering, death, and resurrection,¹⁰ and the Prayer after Communion mentions his death and resurrection.¹¹ The mention of resurrection has to be made in the midst of the focus on suffering and death because the Eucharist is a memorial of the suffering, death, resurrection, ascension, and gift of the Spirit of Jesus. In other words, the Eucharist always celebrates all five aspects of the paschal mystery even if a particular celebration highlights one or two of them; this is fully explored in the chapter on Holy Thursday. The Prayer over the People specifically names the agony of the cross instead of suffering.¹²

REFLECTION

Paschal mystery spirituality is stamped on every page of *The Roman Missal*, but it is more pronounced during Holy Week. The implication is that it should be the way of life for the followers of Jesus Christ. The Sixth Sunday of Lent is Palm Sunday of the Passion of the Lord. While most people focus on getting a palm branch, the procession with leafy greens serves as an entrance to the proclamation of the gospel: an account of the suffering, death, and burial of Jesus according to one of the Synoptic Gospels (Mark, Matthew, Luke). Palm Sunday of the Passion of the Lord begins Holy Week, the most solemn days in the liturgical calendar. Furthermore, it prepares congregants for the Sacred Paschal Triduum, especially the Good Friday of the Passion of the Lord celebration.

Those gathered for Palm Sunday are told to have the same attitude as Jesus, who willingly accepted suffering and death with the trust that God would raise him from the dead. The Eucharist makes it very clear that suffering and death culminate in resurrection. As a type of reverse paradox, the palm branch we get this day was alive not too long before it was cut from a tree, sealed in plastic, and shipped to church. When we get it on Palm Sunday, it is still green and supple. However, in a few hours—and definitely in a few days—it will dry, turn brown, and indicate that it is dead. Thus, the very thing associated with Palm Sunday represents life and death; the palm branch is a sign of paschal mystery spirituality.

9. Ibid., par. 23.
10. Ibid., par. 24.
11. Ibid., par. 26.
12. Ibid., par. 27.

The paradox is even more pronounced when we realize that only John's Gospel mentions "branches of palm trees" (John 12:13). Matthew's Gospel says that people cut branches from unidentified trees (Matt 21:8); Mark's Gospel says that people spread unidentified leafy branches (Mark 11:8); and Luke's Gospel doesn't mention any type of branches (Luke 19:28–40).

1. What do you understand the focus of Palm Sunday to be? In what specific ways does that focus serve to interpret the same aspect of your life?

2. Do you accept suffering and death with trust that God will raise you to new life? What experiences have led you to such trust?

3. In your life, where do you find traces of paschal mystery spirituality? How do those traces help you understand your life experiences?

4. Using the sign of a palm branch, of what life-and-death experience does it remind you?

4

Palm Sunday
Suffering is Betrayal for the Matthean Jesus

WHILE THE CHRONOLOGICAL ORDER of the Synoptic Gospels is Mark, Matthew, and Luke, the biblical order is Matthew, Mark, and Luke. *The Lectionary* follows the biblical order. Thus, Matthew's account of Jesus' suffering, crucifixion, death, and resurrection is read in Year A (2020, 2023, 2026, etc.). *The Lectionary* order is followed here.

Matthew presents Jesus as a betrayed Messiah. He accomplishes this by giving both Peter and Judas larger roles—bigger parts—and by comparing and contrasting them as betrayers. The unique Matthean account of Peter walking on water (Matt 14:28–31) presents Peter as a disciple whose faith is not very stable. It also compliments the scene during the Passover supper in which Peter tells Jesus that even if all the disciples have their faith in him shaken, Peter's will never be (Matt 26:33). It isn't long before Peter betrays Jesus three times, declaring that he does not know the man (Matt 26:72, 74).

Matthew is interested in portraying Peter as a betrayer and then comparing him to Judas, the supreme betrayer. There is no doubt that Peter is a betrayer, but he is not from the same mold as Judas. Judas, identified as "Judas Iscariot who betrayed" Jesus in Matthew's list of twelve disciples (Matt 10:4), goes to the chief priests to set up a plot to betray Jesus for which he will receive thirty pieces of silver (Matt 26:14-16).

During the Passover meal, Jesus identifies Judas as his betrayer. After the Twelve ask about the betrayer Matthew writes, "Judas, who betrayed [Jesus], said, 'Surely not I, Rabbi?' He answered, 'You have said so'" (Matt 26:25). So, with another one of the betrayers clearly identified, it is not long before Jesus is kissed by Judas (Matt 26:47–50); the usual sign of love is turned into the sign of betrayal! Up to this point in Matthew's Gospel, Judas and Peter are alike; both of them have betrayed Jesus.

Unique to Matthew is the story about Judas' regret and suicide. The author records: "When Judas, [Jesus'] betrayer, saw that Jesus was condemned, he repented and brought back the thirty pieces of silver to the chief priests and elders. He said, 'I have sinned by betraying innocent blood.' But they said, 'What is that to us? See to it yourself.' Throwing down the pieces of silver in the temple, he departed; and he went and hanged himself" (Matt 27:3-5).

At this point Matthew switches from his comparison of Peter to Judas to the contrast between the two characters. Both Peter and Judas regret what they do. After Peter denies Jesus three times, Matthew states, "[H]e went out and wept bitterly" (Matt 26:75b). Peter repents of his betrayal of Jesus. Judas regrets what he does, but he does not truly repent. Instead, he betrays himself and commits suicide. According to Matthew's contrast, betrayal does not have to end in despair; a person always has the opportunity to repent.

Matthew portrays Jesus predicting his passion three times. This literary technique, called prediction-fulfillment, is designed to draw the reader deeper and deeper into the story. In other words, it keeps the reader reading to find out if all happens as predicted. The first prediction (Matt 16:21–23) contains the basic idea that Jesus will suffer, be killed, and be raised; the author balances the view of Jesus as the betrayed, suffering, and dead Messiah with the view of him as the risen Lord. In Matthew's transfiguration narrative (Matt 17:1-8), Jesus is portrayed as if he has already been raised from the dead. In the second passion prediction, after Jesus talks about suffering, death, and resurrection the disciples question him about his meaning and are overwhelmed with grief (Matt 17:23). Matthew's record of Jesus' third passion prediction (Matt 20:17-19) is very clear; Jesus will be handed over, condemned to death, mocked, flogged, crucified, and raised on the third day.

In the narrative about the mother of James and John asking for positions of power for her sons, Matthew focuses on drinking the cup of betrayal. Jesus asks the two disciples, "Are you able to drink the cup that I am about to drink?" (Matt 20:22b) After they reply, "We are able," he says, "You will indeed drink my cup . . . " (20:22c–23a). To drink from the cup is a metaphor indicating that a person has accepted God's will. Matthew returns to this theme in the narrative about Jesus' agony in the garden. The author focuses on the cup of suffering—betrayal—which Jesus will drink in order to do the will of his heavenly Father. In the first of his prayers, Jesus says, "My Father, if it is possible, let this cup pass from me; yet not I want but what you want" (26:39). In the second prayer, Jesus says, "My Father, if this cannot pass unless I drink it, your will be done" (26:42). Jesus' third prayer, according to Matthew, is similar (Matt 26:44).

Now the stage is set for Judas's and Peter's betrayal of Jesus, which Matthew views as part of the providential plan of God. Matthew begins his narrative of the final events surrounding Jesus' life with a passion prediction placed on the lips of Jesus: "You know that after two days the Passover is coming, and the Son of Man will be handed over to be crucified" (26:2).

Jesus drinks the cup of betrayal, which leads to suffering and death. After he is crucified, the Matthean Jesus cries out in a loud voice, "My God, my God, why have you forsaken me?" (Matt 27:46) The reference to thinking that he is forsaken is Matthean betrayal. The author portrays Jesus thinking that God has betrayed him. Such a scene could not be but more Matthean irony. God is not found in rescuing, according to Matthew, but God is found exactly where God is not usually thought to be—dying on the cross because of betraying disciples! There is no doubt about who Jesus is; the author makes it clear that he is the "Son of God" (Matt 27:40, 43), who has been betrayed.

The author of Matthew's Gospel makes it clear that trust in God must remain even through betrayal to death. God saves Jesus through his death, not from his death. God will save others the same way that God saved Jesus—through death, not from death. According to Matthew, God is present through betrayal, which leads to suffering and death. In other words, God does not betray his people, even though they, like Jesus, may think he has. God is always faithful and works through betrayal and death.

Betrayal does not have to end in despair as it did for Judas. Once it is experienced, according to Matthew, and the disciple has remained faithful, like Jesus, through it all, a person can still experience new life, like Peter. Matthew makes this clear in his major post-resurrection appearance of Jesus. After the eleven disciples assemble, Jesus commissions them. Since Peter is one of the Twelve, he is included in the eleven. The author writes, "When they saw him, they worshiped him; but some doubted" (28:17). With this line, Matthew vindicates Jesus, whom he had portrayed as thinking that God had betrayed him on the cross. With this line, Matthew vindicates Peter, who not only doubted, but betrayed Jesus. With this line, Matthew vindicates any follower of Jesus who betrays him or is betrayed by another because of faith in Jesus.

Thus, the Matthean account of Jesus' suffering and death read on Palm Sunday of the Passion of the Lord in Cycle A focuses on suffering and death caused by betrayal. The Matthean Jesus demonstrates that trust in God must remain even through betrayal to death. God always has the last word. In Matthew's Gospel, the last word is resurrection.

REFLECTION

According to Matthew's Gospel, God calls people to do his will, even if this means experiencing betrayal, which leads to suffering and death, like Jesus. Only a little time spent reflecting on betrayal will reveal that there is a lot of it in the world. There is self-betrayal, which takes the form of alcohol, drugs, sex, and food addiction; a person betrays himself or herself by denying that he or she has a problem. Betrayal happens between friends. One person entrusts his or her confidence in a trusted friend. Another tells his or her friend a secret from the heart—privileged information to be shared with no one. However, confidence is betrayed when the trusted friend reveals the other's confidence or secret to a third party. Employees betray managers by enriching their business mileage reports, their food allowances, and their time cards. In the world of corporate crime, a gang member betrays another by killing him or her because of dissent. One chairperson blackmails another. One company takes over another because an officer betrays the business. Parents often feel betrayed by their children, who promise to keep the curfew, to do well in high school and college, or to repay a loan, but such promises are not kept.

Could it be that God is at work in these experiences of betrayal, like the author of Matthew's Gospel portrays God at work in Jesus' life? Could it be that God is found to be exactly where one does not think that God should be? Matthew's Gospel answers both of those questions by saying, "Yes!"

1. How does Matthew's presentation of suffering and death as the result of betrayal intersect with your life? When have you most recently felt betrayed by God?

2. When have you most recently betrayed another person or yourself? How was God revealed in your experience? When have you most recently been betrayed by another person? How was God revealed in your experience?

3. In your life, identify one experience in which you did God's will, was (felt) betrayed by God and/or others, suffered, died, and discovered new life?

4. How does Matthew introduce resurrection into his passion—suffering and death—predictions? When have you known that new life would be the result of your suffering and death?

5. Is it God's will that Jesus be betrayed and suffer and die in Matthew's Gospel? What are the implications of your answer for your paschal mystery spirituality?

6. If God saves Jesus from betrayal through death, how has he saved you from betrayl through death?

7. What are your thoughts and feelings about the principal theme of betrayal leading to suffering and death in Matthew's Gospel?

8. How does Matthew's theme of betrayal fit into your paschal mystery spirituality?

5

Palm Sunday
Suffering is Abandonment for the Markan Jesus

MOST SCRIPTURE SCHOLARS ACCEPT Mark's Gospel as the oldest of those found in the Christian Bible (New Testament) and date it around 70 CE. The account of Jesus' suffering and death in Mark is read in Cycle B (2018, 2021, 2024, etc.) on Palm Sunday of the Passion of the Lord. The primary theme that runs through Mark's narrative is abandonment. The unknown author most likely wrote this narrative to strengthen the faith of those followers of Jesus of Nazareth who were being abandoned by others in the face of persecution.

The author understands Jesus to be a tragic hero. The gospel is a tragedy, as the hero of the story, Jesus, a Jew, is killed by the Romans, who are the conquerors and occupiers of Jesus' native land. One of the gospel's basic theses is that a follower of Jesus of Nazareth will experience abandonment, just like Jesus did on the cross. Suffering is abandonment according to this first-century author.

To see how the author handles this theme, one needs to examine the structural arrangement of the gospel. The author introduces the abandonment theme with the call of the fishermen Simon and Andrew, who abandon their nets and follow Jesus (Mark 1:16–18). Then, he calls James and John, who abandon their father and hired men and follow him (Mark 1:19–20). Later, he calls Levi while he is sitting at his tax booth, and he follows him (Mark 2:14). Thus is established the fact that Jesus' apostles are good at abandonment!

The pivot point of the gospel is Peter's confession to Jesus, "You are the messiah" (Mark 8:29b), and Jesus' ensuing rebuke of Peter. After this scene the theme of Jesus being powerful in word and deed, which is established in the first half of Mark's Gospel, is reversed. The scene is set on the road to Caesarea Philippi. As they are walking, Jesus asks his disciples, who have heard his powerful words and witnesses his powerful deeds but not determined who Jesus is, "Who do people say that I am?" (Mark 8:27) The disciples give three wrong answers! When Jesus asks, "But who do you say that I am?" Peter steps forward and declares, "You are the messiah" (Mark 8:29b). However, Peter's answer affirms a messiah of powerful words and powerful deeds.

Jesus immediately begins to teach the disciples "that the Son of Man must undergo great suffering, and be rejected by the elders, the chief priests, and the scribes, and be killed, and after three days rise again" (Mark 8:31). This type of language has never been used before in this gospel. It is no wonder, then, that Peter takes Jesus aside and begins to rebuke him (Mark 8:32). But Jesus turns around and, looking at all his disciples, rebukes Peter by saying: "Get behind me, Satan. For you are setting your mind not on divine things but on human things" (Mark 8:33). In other words, Peter tells Jesus that he has the idea of discipleship all wrong. It is not about suffering, rejection, death, and resurrection, but about being powerful in words and deeds. Peter needs to be exorcised of his idea that discipleship involves power.

Summoning a crowd from nowhere, as this author fondly does, Jesus begins to teach his disciples and the crowd this new perspective. He says, "If any want to become my followers, let them deny themselves and take up their cross and follow me" (Mark 8:34). Discipleship is now defined as powerlessness, which includes suffering, rejection, and death on a cross! In one word, powerlessness is abandonment. This is confirmed by the transfiguration scene which follows and gives a glimpse of what awaits those who undergo abandonment on the other side of death. While Jesus, Peter, James, and John are coming down from the mountain after the experience of the transfiguration and are engaged in discussion, Mark editorializes that Jesus "ordered them to tell no one about what they had seen, until after the Son of Man had risen from the dead" (Mark 9:12). This is Mark's post-resurrection appearance of Jesus, since he presents none at the end of his good news.

Now, the author vividly presents his new perspective that suffering is a willingness to experience abandonment, which leads to death, in his passion account. He incorporates two more predictions of Jesus' suffering and death. In the first, Jesus teaches his disciples that he will be handed over to men and they will kill him, and three days after his death he will rise (Mark 9:31). In the second, as Jesus and his disciples get closer to Jerusalem, he tells them that he will be handed over, condemned to death, scourged, put to death, and rise after three days (Mark 10:33–34). In between these predictions, Jesus' disciples are characterized as foolish, uncomprehending followers (Mark 9:32).

Jesus asks James and John, "Are you able to drink the cup that I drink, or be baptized with the baptism that I am baptized with?" (Mark 10:38b) Drinking the cup is a Hebrew Bible (Old Testament) metaphor for accepting the will of God. Jesus accepts the will of God, which according to Mark is abandonment leading to suffering and death. Also, the author makes clear that he considers baptism to be an immersion into abandonment leading to suffering and death. At this point the reader should be fully aware that discipleship involves no power but plenty of powerlessness at the hand of God!

Discipleship also involves willingly accepting the suffering and death which is the result of abandonment. Mark's Jesus is the model of how this is done. In the garden, he prays, "Abba, Father, for you all things are possible; remove this cup away from me; yet, not what I want, but what you want" (Mark 14:36). This prayer, said three times, emphasizes that only God is all-powerful. Human beings, including Jesus of Nazareth, are powerless when faced with the cup, a reference to the story about the ambition of James and John and the ensuing teaching about accepting the will of God, even if it entails abandonment to suffering and death. God's will takes precedence over human will, even over the human will of Jesus. God's will is that Jesus suffers, dies, and be raised, as has been predicted three times throughout the second half of the gospel.

The author brings the abandonment dimension into his theme in the scene of the arrest of Jesus, which follows the garden scene. After Judas identifies Jesus with a kiss to the crowd with swords and clubs who had come from the chief priests, the scribes, and the elders (Mark 14:43), Mark makes it clear that all the disciples "deserted him and fled" (Mark 14:50). This is the last time that the disciples are mentioned in this gospel except for Peter.

During the Passover supper, Peter tells Jesus that even if all the other disciples should have their faith shaken, his will not be. Then, the author records Jesus saying to Peter that he will deny him three times before the cock crows two times. Peter, however, vehemently states that he would never deny Jesus (Mark 14:29–31). However, after Jesus is arrested, Mark writes that Peter followed him at a distance into the high priest's courtyard and was seated with the guards, warming himself at the fire (Mark 14:54). It is not long before Peter fulfills Jesus' prediction of Peter's threefold denial of him. Mark records:

> While Peter was below in the courtyard, one of the servant-girls of the high priest came by. When she saw Peter warming himself, she stared at him and said, "You also were with Jesus, the man from Nazareth." But he denied it, saying, "I do not know or understand what you are talking about." And he went out into the forecourt. Then the cock crowed. And the servant-girl, on seeing him, began again to say to the bystanders, "This man is one of them." But again he denied it. Then after a little while the bystanders again said to Peter, "Certainly you are one of them; for you are a Galilean." But he began to curse, and he swore an oath, "I do not know this man you are talking about." At that moment the cock crowed for the second time. (Mark 14:66–72a)

After this, Peter disappears, like the rest of the disciples, from Mark's Gospel.

To further emphasize abandonment the author includes a curious story about a young man who followed Jesus "wearing nothing but a linen cloth" (Mark 14:51). Those who had come to take Jesus into custody "caught hold of him, but he left the cloth and ran off naked" (Mark 14:51-52). This account serves as a red flag for the reader, who will have to wait until the final verses of the gospel to have the sign of the naked young man interpreted for him or her. The point of the story is that Jesus is abandoned even by an unnamed man wearing only his underwear!

Abandonment culminates with the final suffering and death of Jesus on the cross. After his trial, the sentence of death, the struggle to carry the cross with the help of Simon—a Cyrenian—the crucifixion, and the taunting from the bystanders, the Markan Jesus utters his final words, "My God, my God, why have you forsaken me?" (Mark 15:34) Jesus, who in the garden had prayed to do the will of God, is portrayed as thinking that in his final moments even God has abandoned him. All of his disciples abandoned him. After his burial only powerless women, Mary Magdalene and Mary the mother of Joses, see where he is buried (Mark 15:47). The humanity of Jesus shines through in this scene. It is a humanity which the disciples could not understand. It is a humanity which the reader finds difficult to understand.

God's will is not yet complete, however. The reader has been reminded three times that after experiencing suffering and death, which flow from abandonment, Jesus would be raised from the dead. And so the proclamation comes three days after Jesus' death and burial from "a young man, dressed in a white robe, sitting on the right side [of the tomb]" (Mark 16:5). The proclamation to three women, who in the culture of the time would represent powerlessness, is this: " . . . [Y]ou are looking for Jesus of Nazareth, who was crucified. He has been raised; he is not here" (Mark 16:6ab).

The reader immediately recognizes the young man as the one who fled away naked, leaving his white linen cloth behind, after Jesus was arrested. Now, what is he doing in the tomb? What statement is the author making about resurrection and the abandonment which led to suffering and death preceding it?

The young man is an "abandoner." For Mark he represents the disciples, the reader, and anyone else who willingly experiences abandonment which leads to suffering and death. For Mark the young man is a sign of what Mark understands resurrection to be—a trust that God is present even when it seems like God is absent. In other words, in the deepest moment of the experience of abandonment, where God is not usually thought to be, this is where God is to be found, remaining faithful to those who are faithful to God's will.

The resurrection, as far as Mark is concerned, is grounded in the experience of abandonment, which is what his audience was facing. The young man, who had run away naked, now appears in the tomb dressed in a white robe. He has been baptized into abandonment, powerlessness, and has been initiated into a new way of life. It is likely, according to Mark, that he will have to suffer, like Jesus, for his faith.

Mark is exhorting his audience not to understand abandonment which leads to suffering and death as negative. The experience of it is a baptism, a drinking from the cup, like Jesus. The possibility for faith occurs at the moment of abandonment. Even though people abandon each other,

God never abandons anyone—not even his own Son, who thought that God had abandoned him, when he hung dying on a cross!

Mark takes the existential experience of his audience and says that it is the same existential experience of Jesus of Nazareth. What happened to Jesus is what is happening to his followers after 70 CE. However, God raised the abandoned Jesus from the dead. Those who are abandoned after 70 CE will share in the same fate, according to the author, if they do the will of God. Indeed, the true family of Jesus is those who do the will of God (Mark 3:35).

The author of this gospel understands that a person cannot believe until he or she has been baptized into abandonment. To abandon another person is like dying, which is, hopefully, followed by repentance, faith, and new life. When one experiences this terrifying event, he or she feels abandoned by God, who is present when in usual human reasoning God is determined to be absent. Furthermore, when one experiences abandonment, there are usually no witnesses. Likewise, in Mark's Gospel the resurrection has already taken place when the women arrive at the tomb. No one witnesses the resurrection. Why? Because it is an event which cannot be witnessed; it transcends the ordinary. Transformation cannot be seen; only the results are visible in the life of the transformed.

There are no post-resurrection appearances by the Markan Jesus. If the narrative is followed carefully, the reader can conclude why the author could not have presented any. Resurrection implies power—the power of God—and this would undermine the whole of the second half of Mark's Gospel, which has attempted to present discipleship as modeled by Jesus of Nazareth, the Son of God, as powerless abandonment which leads to suffering and death. So, the gospel originally ended with the women going out of and fleeing from the tomb, seized with terror and amazement (Mark 16:8a). Mark's final sentence is this: " . . . [T]hey said nothing to anyone, for they were afraid" (Mark 16:8b).

The confirmation of Mark's definition of discipleship as a willingness to experience abandonment, which leads to suffering and death, is found in the verses immediately following the account of Jesus' death. Mark states, "[W]hen the centurion, who stood facing [Jesus] saw that in this way he breathed his last, he said, 'Truly this man was God's Son!'" (Mark 15:39) There is much Markan irony here. First, since all Jesus' disciples have abandoned him and he has died all alone, it takes a Roman centurion finally to state what the reader has heard as a voice from the sky at Jesus' baptism and at his transfiguration: " . . . [T]his man was God's Son" (Mark 15:39). Second, this line not only echoes those two previous stories, but it serves as the confirmation that being the Son of God and doing God's will for Jesus meant accepting abandonment which led to his suffering and death.

For the author of this gospel, it is the experience of abandonment leading to suffering and death which is redemptive. Resurrection is the confirmation of God's faithfulness. Abandonment to suffering and death is the confirmation of the modern disciple's faithfulness. Mark ends his gospel with a proclamation of the resurrection by the young man in the tomb with the abandonment which leads to suffering and death clearly etched upon the reader's mind. The reader should have no doubt about the meaning of discipleship or paschal mystery spirituality.

REFLECTION

If we look at the human situations of powerlessness in which we often find ourselves, we see the accuracy of Mark's theme of abandonment. For example, abandonment takes place in adultery. One spouse abandons another. If repentance and reconciliation occur, faith in the other becomes possible again, and both husband and wife rise from the dead to new life. Friendships are often destroyed by gossip, anger, and misunderstandings. One friend abandons another. But if one dares to approach the other in repentance, the possibility of faith in the relationship occurs, and both friends rise from the death of their relationship to its new life. Accidents leave people feeling abandoned. When someone we love is injured or killed in a plane, train, car, or bus accident, we feel abandoned. Likewise, the injured party often feels abandoned, while he or she recuperates in a hospital bed for weeks or is confined to a wheelchair for the rest of his or her life.

Almost every person abandons God. The experience might be one of stealing, cheating, lying, killing, coveting, failing to worship, cursing, etc. Sin is abandoning God. We abandon God when we rely upon ourselves for what we need and erroneously believe that we can save ourselves. In such moments of abandonment, we hit the depths of our human powerlessness, where we do not think that God is to be found. But it is there where we meet the faithful, forgiving God, who willed his own Son to die and demonstrated faithfulness by raising him from the dead. In our moments of powerlessness, we come to faith and are raised from the depths of our humanity to the heights of new life. Powerlessness leads to abandonment,

Christ Our Passover Has Been Sacrificed

which results in suffering and death. Faith trusts that God will remain faithful, even when people may not, and raise the abandoned sufferer to new life.

1. When have you most recently found yourself seeking power, like Peter, because you believe that power is the way of discipleship? How was that idea changed for you?

2. When have you most recently felt abandoned by God? Who left: You or God? When have you most recently abandoned another person? How was reconciliation accomplished? What new life ensued after this experience?

3. In your life, identify one experience in which you did God's will, was (felt) abandoned by God and/or others, suffered, died, and discovered new life?

4. How does the author of Mark's Gospel work out his theme that abandonment leads to suffering, death, and new life? What does the author understand new life (resurrection) to be? Identify an experience in your life that illustrates the theme that abandonment leads to suffering, death, and new life.

5. What are your thoughts and feelings about the principal theme—suffering is abandonment—found in Mark's Gospel?

6. How does abandonment fit into your paschal mystery spirituality?

6

Palm Sunday
Suffering is Martyrdom for the Lukan Jesus

LUKE PRESENTS THE LIFE of a follower of Jesus as a journey through suffering and death to resurrection. Jesus is portrayed as the first martyr and a model for others. For the author of this gospel, suffering is martyrdom, an event which may have been all too common for the members of his audience near the end of the first century CE. The author of Luke's Gospel demonstrates that the suffering endured by Jesus and leading to his martyrdom precedes his resurrection and ascension into glory. If the Christian wishes to share in Jesus' resurrection and glory, he or she must be willing to participate in the suffering which leads to martyrdom, like Jesus. By looking at Luke's unique material in his gospel, one can see how his theological perspective concerning suffering emerges.

A major portion of Luke's Gospel (9:51—19:45) is set on the road to Jerusalem. The reader is prepared for these ten chapters in the transfiguration account, which precedes the first indication of the journey to Jerusalem. Luke uniquely notes that Moses and Elijah appear in glory to Jesus and that they speak of his exodus that he is going to accomplish in Jerusalem (Luke 9:31). Luke has employed the reference to the exodus, the key Hebrew Bible (Old Testament) event of Israel's escape from Egypt and given it a new meaning. Now, it refers to Jesus' suffering, death, and resurrection, which are accomplished in Jerusalem. In other words, Luke makes it clear that Jesus' willingness to journey through suffering and death will end with a great escape into glory, as portrayed in Luke's unique narratives about Jesus' ascension (Luke 24:51; Acts 1:6-12).

As the Lukan Jesus travels along (Luke 13:22, 33; 17:11; 18:31; 19:28), he tells parables, heals the sick, and teaches. After Jesus' death, resurrection, and ascension (Luke 24:50–53; Acts 1:6–12) in Jerusalem, the gift of the Spirit is given to the apostles (Acts 2:1–13) and the journey continues in Luke's second volume, the Acts of the Apostles, through the adventures of Peter and Paul.

Luke is a master at editorializing, especially when it comes to presenting Jesus as a model pray-er. The author believes that through prayer a follower of Jesus is strengthened to continue his or her journey through suffering and death to martyrdom. Prayer reveals the innocence of the sufferer; that is, prayer uncovers the martyr. Thus, before every major event Luke portrays Jesus at prayer. After Jesus is baptized, Luke writes that he was praying (Luke 3:21). Before he chooses the Twelve, Luke records that Jesus spent the night in prayer to God (Luke 6:12). Luke introduces the narrative concerning Peter's confession of Jesus as the Messiah of God (Luke 9:20) after he describes Jesus praying in solitude (Luke 8:18). In the account of the transfiguration, the author makes it clear that Jesus went up the mountain to pray and that it was while he was praying that his face changed in appearance and his clothing became dazzling white (Luke 9:28–29). After the Passover supper, the Lukan Jesus tells Peter that he has prayed that Peter's faith may not fail (Luke 22:32). In the gospel, praying reaches its peak with Jesus saying, "Father, forgive them; for they do not know what they are doing" (Luke 23:34), while he is being crucified. Then, Luke presents Jesus' final words as a prayer: "Father, into your hands I commend my spirit" (Luke 23:46).

Those last words serve two important Lukan functions. First, Jesus returns to God the Spirit he had received at his conception (Luke 1:35) so that it can be poured out on his apostles at Pentecost (Acts 2:1-4). Second, the Lukan Jesus' final words complete the portrait of Jesus as an innocent martyr. Only in this gospel does Pilate three times declare Jesus to be innocent. Addressing the chief priests and the crowds, the Lukan Pilate says that he finds Jesus not guilty (Luke 23:4). Addressing the chief priests, the rulers, and the people, Pilate declares that after conducting his investigation he finds Jesus not guilty of the charges they have brought against him (Luke 23:14). After the crowd calls for the release of Barabbas, Pilate says that he has found Jesus guilty of no capital crime (Luke 23:22). After being sent to Herod, a unique scene in this gospel, the reader is told through Pilate that Jesus is innocent (Luke 23:15). Even one of the criminals, who is crucified with Jesus and who is given a speaking part by Luke, declares that Jesus has done nothing criminal (Luke 23:41). And finally the centurion says, "Certainly this man was innocent" (Luke 23:47). According to Luke, followers of Jesus are to imitate him in innocence. Their prayer will strengthen them throughout their journey through suffering and death to martyrdom.

While Luke sustains his prayer-on-the-journey through suffering and death motif, he also presents three predictions of Jesus' passion and resurrection. The first prediction of Jesus suffering and death follows the Lukan Peter's confession about Jesus. After Peter confesses that Jesus is the Messiah of God (Luke 9:20), Jesus says that he must suffer greatly and be rejected by the elders, the chief priests, and the scribes, and be killed and on the third day be raised (Luke 9:22). Luke's second prediction of Jesus suffering and death follows his account of the transfiguration and the healing of a boy with an unclean spirit. Luke records Jesus telling his disciples to pay attention to the fact that he will be handed over to men (Luke 9:43-44). A minor, unique passion prediction is found in the Lukan Jesus' discourse about being prepared for the day the Son of Man is revealed (Luke 17:30). Jesus says that he must suffer greatly and be rejected by this generation (Luke 17:25). Luke's third passion prediction is placed in the middle of his journey-to-Jerusalem section. After narrating the story about the rich official and the teaching about riches and renunciation (Luke 18:18-30), Jesus says, "See, we are going up to Jerusalem, and everything that is written about the Son of Man by the prophets will be accomplished. For he will be handed over to the Gentiles; and he will be mocked and insulted and spat upon. After they have flogged him, they will kill him, and on the third day he will rise again" (Luke 18:31b-33).

The fulfillment aspect of the schema occurs in the post-resurrection accounts. Unique to Luke's narrative about the women at the tomb is the statement made to the women by the two men in dazzling garments (Luke 24:4): "Remember how he told you, while he was still in Galilee, that the Son of Man must be handed over to sinners, and be crucified, and on the third day rise again" (Luke 24:6-7). A second fulfillment is found in Luke's unique narrative about Jesus' appearance to the two disciples on the road to

Emmaus. In this story, the unrecognized, risen Jesus admonishes his fellow travelers: "Oh, how foolish you are, and how slow of heart to believe all that the prophets have declared! Was it not necessary that the Messiah should suffer these things and then enter into his glory?" (Luke 24:25–26) The author then editorializes, "... [B]eginning with Moses and all the prophets, he interpreted to them the things about himself in all the scriptures" (Luke 24:27). After narrating the second appearance of the risen Jesus, Luke provides the third fulfillment aspect of his prediction-fulfillment motif. The Lukan Jesus tells his disciples, "These are my words that I spoke to you while I was still with you—that everything written about me in the law of Moses, the prophets, and the psalms must be fulfilled. Thus it is written, that the Messiah is to suffer and to rise from the dead on the third day" (Luke 24:44, 46).

Luke assigns Peter the role of hero. Luke does present Peter as a betrayer, but the Lukan Jesus predicts that Peter will repent and become the leader of the disciples. The Lukan Jesus tells him that all the apostles will be sifted like wheat, but Jesus has prayed that Peter's faith may not fail. Once Peter repents, Jesus tells him to strengthen his brothers. Peter responds that he is prepared to go to prison to die with Jesus (Luke 22:31–33), but Jesus says, "I tell you, Peter, the cock will not crow this day, until you have denied three times that you know me" (Luke 22:34).

Luke gathers together into one narrative (Luke 22:54–62) the references to Peter's following Jesus at a distance after Jesus' arrest and Peter's actual denial of Jesus. Luke, however, portrays Peter within sight of Jesus, as Peter three times acknowledges that he does not know Jesus. Luke writes, "The Lord turned and looked at Peter," who "went out and wept bitterly" (Luke 22:61a, 62).

As Luke predicts, Peter returns. In the author's scene of the women at the tomb, after the women announce the resurrection to the eleven, Luke narrates that Peter got up and ran to the tomb, saw the burial cloths, and went home amazed at what had happened (Luke 24:12). Also, after the two disciples on the road to Emmaus return to Jerusalem they are greeted by the eleven with the statement that Christ has been raised and that he appeared to Simon (Luke 24:34). However, Luke never records the event of the appearance of Jesus to Simon.

Luke maintains that Jesus was betrayal by Judas. However, he makes it clear that Satan entered into Judas, called Iscariot, and he went to the chief priests and temple guards to discuss a plan for handing over Jesus to them. They were pleased and agreed to pay him money. He accepted their offer and sought a favorable opportunity to hand him over to them in the absence of a crowd (Luke 22:3-6). Some of Judas' guilt is removed by Luke's note about Satan entering into him.

Luke narrates the story about Judas' plot to hand over Jesus to the chief priests and the scribes (Luke 22:1-6), the preparations for the Passover (Luke 11:7-13), the Passover supper (Luke 22:14-20), and Jesus' prediction that the hand of the betrayer was on the table (Luke 22:21). For Luke, sharing a meal with Jesus is not an indication of authentic discipleship. All of the disciples are present for the Lukan institution of the Eucharist narrative, yet both Judas and Peter betray Jesus. Later, when Judas hands over Jesus, Luke notes that Judas leads a crowd. He goes to Jesus to kiss him, and Jesus asks him if he is betraying him with a kiss (Luke 22:47-48).

It is important to notice another reference to Satan. When predicting Peter's betrayal, Jesus tells him, as noted above, that Satan has demanded to sift all of the apostles like wheat (Luke 22:31). Using this and other references to Satan, Luke fulfills his unique prophecy made after Jesus three temptations (Luke 4:1-13): "When the devil had finished every test, he departed from him until an opportune time" (Luke 4:13). Thus, Jesus successfully overcomes Satan's temptations, while Judas and Peter cannot (Luke 22:31-32, 53). This means that Peter, like Judas, has his guilt exculpated. His action of betrayal is blamed on Satan.

The reader is not told what happened to Judas until the Acts of the Apostles. Luke records Peter relating what happened to Judas. According to Peter's speech, Judas bought a parcel of land, and falling headlong, he burst open in the middle, and all his insides spilled out (Acts 1:17-18).

In Luke's account of Jesus' visit to the Mount of Olives before his betrayal by Judas and ensuing arrest, twice he tells his disciples to pray that they may not undergo the test (Luke 22:40, 46). The test is the temptation to be lured away from discipleship. Jesus prays, "Father, if you are willing, remove this cup from me; yet, not my will but yours be done" (Luke 22:42). Immediately following Jesus' exhortation to Peter about vigilant and faithful servants, Jesus says, "I have a baptism with which to be baptized, and what stress I am under until it is completed!" (Luke 12:50) This baptism refers to his death. Luke does not connect the cup, baptism, suffering, and death. For Luke, the cup is a reference to Eucharist, which by the time he was writing this gospel—90-100 CE—was already being celebrated as a memorial of the suffering, death, and resurrection of Jesus. This becomes clear in the unique Lukan mention of two cups during the Passover meal. The author records what Jesus did:

> ... He took a cup, and after giving thanks he said [to the apostles], "Take this and divide it among yourselves...." Then he took a loaf of bread, and when he had given thanks, he broke it and gave it to them, saying, "This is my body, which is given for you. Do this in remembrance of me." And he did the same with the cup after supper, saying, "This cup that is poured out for you is the new covenant in my blood." (Luke 22:17, 19–20)

It is no accident, then, that in his post-resurrection stories Luke portrays Jesus as eating with those to whom he appears. After walking with the two disciples on the road to Emmaus, the risen Christ sits down at table with them, takes bread, says the blessing, breaks it, and gives it to them. And with that gesture their eyes are opened and they recognize him (Luke 24:30–31). When they get back to Jerusalem, they tell the other disciples how he was made known to them in the breaking of the bread (Luke 24:35).

Then, Jesus appears again. The disciples give him a piece of baked fish which he takes and eats in front of them (Luke 24:42–43). Immediately Jesus reminds them that he was supposed to die and rise (Luke 24:46). The action of eating—breaking bread and remembering the suffering, death, and resurrection of Jesus—is a theme woven throughout Luke's Gospel (Luke 5:29; 7:36; 11:37–54; 14:1, 15–24; 15:1–32;19:1–10). In Luke's community, Jesus' suffering, death, and resurrection are remembered when a cup is poured and bread is broken. It is important to note that the outcast of society—tax collectors, the poor, the handicapped, the wanderers, and the lost—are those who share Jesus' table, not to mention his opponents: the Pharisees.

There is one final, unique Lukan trait in the Mount of Olives scene which needs to be mentioned. Luke writes that Jesus, "[i]n his anguish ... prayed more earnestly, and his sweat became like great drops of blood falling down on the ground" (Luke 22:44). Rothschild notes that it is often thought "that this passage describes Jesus as sweating blood. This is not the case. The word 'like' indicates that blood is a metaphor for the copiousness—and perhaps the viscosity and color—of Jesus perspiration."[1] This Lukan editorial comment serves to connect the Passover supper cups and the death of the innocent Jesus on the cross. When Luke's community shared

---

1. Rothschild, "Holy Sweat," 189.

bread and wine together, they remembered the suffering, death, and resurrection of their Lord, which Luke uniquely refers to as the new covenant (Luke 22:20).

The Lukan Jesus is followed by a large crowd of people (Luke 23:27). After Jesus' death, the author narrates that all the people, who had gathered for the spectacle of his death, went home beating their breasts. However, all his acquaintances stood at a distance, including the women who had followed him from Galilee and saw these events (Luke 23:48–49).

The Lukan Jesus cannot save himself, even though some of those around him tempt him to do so (Luke 23:35–37, 39). Jesus, of course, cannot save himself—only God does that. However, Jesus does save the one repentant criminal (Luke 23:42–43). God saves Jesus by raising him from the dead. Luke's unique two men in dazzling garments (Luke 24:4) tell three women that he is not in the tomb because he has been raised (Luke 24:6). For Luke, the resurrection is God's vindication of God's supreme martyr, Jesus. The Lukan women go and tell this to the apostles. It is not long before Peter is declaring that God raised him, releasing him from death (Acts 2:24; 3:15, 4:10; 5:30–31).

For Luke discipleship consists of witnessing to what God has done. Such witnessing may lead to suffering and death and, consequentially, martyrdom. However, those who hear the word of God and act on it (Luke 8:21) will be vindicated by God, as was Jesus. In a unique beatitude, the author makes it clear that one must hear the word of God and do it (Luke 11:28). The acting, doing, or observing the word of God is witnessing. The Lukan Jesus states that this must be done daily through self-denial and taking up the cross (Luke 9:23; 14:27). The example of the one who picks up the cross and follows Jesus is a certain Simon, a Cyrenian, who, Luke writes, had Jesus' cross laid on him and was made to carry it behind Jesus (Luke 23:26).

Discipleship means taking the position of servant. After sharing his last supper with his disciples, the Lukan Jesus teaches them that the greatest is the youngest, and the leader is the servant. He reminds them that he has been among them as one who serves (Luke 26–27).

All of this fulfills the Lukan Jesus' instruction to his disciples before he is taken up to heaven. He reminds them that the messiah was supposed to suffer and rise from the dead on the third day and that they are witnesses to those events (Luke 24:46–48).

Another Lukan feature is the discipleship attributed to women. Luke portrays women as disciples, true followers of Jesus. Besides the Twelve, the author states that some women, such as Mary, called Magdalene, Joanna, the wife of Herod's steward Chuza, Susanna, and many others, provided for Jesus and his apostles out of their own resources (Luke 8:2-3). When Jesus is crucified, Luke adds all Jesus' acquaintances to the list (Luke 23:49) along with the women, who watch where Jesus is buried. He also provides a reason for their return to the tomb three days later by mentioning the women, who had come from Galilee with Jesus, see the way in which his body is laid in the tomb, and so they went to prepare spices and perfumed oils (Luke 23:55-56). At the tomb receiving the announcement of the resurrection Luke places Mary Magdalene, Joanna, and Mary the mother of James (Luke 24:10). The mention of Joanna serves to confirm the discipleship of the women and to echo the earlier reference to Joanna, the wife of Herod's steward Chuza (Luke 8:3).

Suffering and death in martyrdom, which is the result of discipleship—witnessing—is not caused by sin, according to Luke. Suffering and death, the result of discipleship, is on a different plane. In Luke's community those who follow Jesus can almost be assured that they will be called upon to witness, to bear fruit through perseverance (Luke 8:15). By their perseverance, like Jesus, they secure their lives (Luke 21:19) and are vindicated by God. Their faithfulness does not result in eternal death.

REFLECTION

Following Jesus, being a disciple, is a journey of a lifetime. While on this journey, "we discover ourselves in discovering God, and discover God in discovering our true self hidden in God."[2] True self subsists in God's eternal love. The journey consists of daily witnessing, which leads to suffering and death—martyrdom. It is living like one is carrying a cross daily. Throughout the world there are many people who conform to the Lukan Jesus' discipleship mold. In 1989, when the Germans finally stood up for the value of unity between East Germany and West Germany, the Berlin Wall tumbled down. Daily, some people witnessed, suffered, and died for their cause. But for thirty years all Germans have lived a new life united as one country. No one can forget the picture of the young person standing in front of the tank in Tiananmen Square in 1989. In such defiance this person made incarnate the desire to overthrow oppression and win democratic freedom. It was not accomplished, but the whole world witnessed the witness—the

---

2. Finley, "Discovering Self."

Palm Sunday

suffering—that this person represented for all young men and women of Beijing, China. The people of the Baltic Republics witnessed for their independence and freedom from the Soviet Union for years. They were willing to be imprisoned, tortured, and killed. Because they never gave up when faced with suffering and death, they bask in the light of independence and freedom today.

A witness for the value of economic justice can be seen in picket lines. Laborers, who go on strike because they believe that they are being treated unjustly by their employers, willingly take cuts in their paychecks, risk losing their jobs, and often are sneered at by those laborers who cross the picket line. Witnessing almost always leads to suffering. It may also lead to death, as it did for Archbishop Oscar Romero in 1980. He is hailed as a martyr for El Salvador. He spoke out against his government's lack of justice. He witnessed to the way of Jesus. He was shot while celebrating the Eucharist. Add to his martyrdom that of the rape and martyrdom of the four church women in 1980—Maura Clarke, Jean Donovan, Ita Ford, and Dorothy Kazel—and the six Jesuit priests in 1989—Ignacio Martin-Baro, Ignacio Ellacuria, Segundo Montes, Juan Moreno, Amando Lopez, and Joaquin Lopez y Lopez—and their housekeeper and her daughter—Elba Ramos and Mariset Ramos—and the troop of witnesses to the way of life of Jesus just keeps increasing.

In the midst of our violent world, we can find many witnesses. Those who keep vigil outside the death chambers of penitentiaries when someone is being executed are witnesses who call for an end to the death penalty. Those who sit in front of abortion clinics are witnesses who demonstrate the value of unborn life. In nursing homes we can find those who care for the elderly and the incapacitated; they witness to the value of life in the golden years.

Every time we gather around the Lord's table we remember that what happened to Jesus is happening to us. The new covenant which he sealed in his blood is ours through baptism. From the table we are sent to witness to the values for which Jesus died. To the table we are called to share with the poor, the outcast, and the sinners. It is at the table that we are strengthened so that we will not betray Jesus, like Judas. There are times that we fail, like Peter. We might say that we don't know Jesus and his way, when the going gets tough and we are faced with suffering and death as a result of our witnessing. But we can repent and return, like Peter, and drink again from the cup.

Through our suffering and death, prayer will strengthen us, as it strengthened Jesus. Prayer enables us to persevere, to remain innocent, and to be prepared for vindication by God. Jesus is our model of discipleship. He heard the word of God and he observed it. His witness to this word led to his suffering, death, and resurrection—his paschal mystery. As his followers, can we expect anything less?

1. If you were arrested on the charge of being a follower of Jesus, what evidence could be produced to convict you?

2. How does Luke think prayer strengthens you for martyrdom? When have you most recently discovered that prayer can strengthen you in your lifetime journey of witnessing?

3. When have you most recently felt that you have been martyred? What new life ensued after this experience?

4. In your life, identify one experience in which you heard God's word and put it into practice. What suffering was involved in this experience? What new life did you discover?

5. What response do you make to Luke's presentation of Judas as a puppet in God's hands? Have you ever experienced anything similar?

6. What do you think of Luke's idea of baptism as a martyr's death?

7. What are your thoughts and feelings about the principal theme—suffering is martyrdom—found in Luke's Gospel?

8. How does martyrdom fit into your paschal mystery spirituality?

7

Thursday of the Lord's Supper

As stated above, The Sacred Paschal Triduum, which intently focuses on the paschal mystery,[1] begins with the Evening Mass of the Lord's Supper on Holy Thursday. One emphasis of this Mass is the institution of the Eucharist, which, as will be seen, is the celebration of the paschal mystery. The Entrance Antiphon mentions the cross, which brought resurrection.[2] The Collect recalls the evening before Jesus handed himself over to death—a reference to the last supper in the Synoptic Gospels (Mark, Matthew, Luke)—and his entrusting a new sacrifice, a banquet of love, to the church.[3] This means that paschal mystery spirituality is alive, present, and active in those who celebrate Eucharist. The Prayer over the Offerings declares that when the sacrifice of the Eucharist is celebrated, the work of redemption is made present and accomplished.[4] The Preface names Christ the true and eternal priest, who instituted the pattern of the everlasting sacrifice, he

---

1. *Roman Missal*, "Universal Norms," par. 18.
2. Ibid., "Thursday of the Lord's Supper: At the Evening Mass," par. 6.
3. Ibid., par. 8.
4. Ibid., par. 15.

being the first to offer himself as the victim and commanding all to make the same offering of his body and blood under the forms of bread and wine.[5]

The Eucharist is the Christian celebration of the Passover. Before Jesus' death, Mark (14:1-2, 12-25), Matthew (26:1-2, 17-29), and Luke (22:1-2, 7-23) record that he celebrates the Passover supper with his disciples. Jesus remembers the escape of his people from slavery and their march to freedom. He recalls their passing over from imminent death to life. After his death and resurrection, it is easy to see why Jesus' disciples began to remember his passover from death to life by sharing a meal of bread and wine. The Hebrew Passover served as the interpretive model for Jesus' suffering, death, and resurrection. Thus, Jesus passed over.

John's Gospel does not contain a narrative about Jesus sharing a Passover supper with his disciples. As already stated above, John records the death of Jesus as taking place on the cross at the same time as the Passover lambs were being slaughtered in the temple. In Johannine understanding, Jesus is the new passover lamb; he replaces the previous one. His blood redeems the world as he passes over from death to life.

To make this connection and interpretation, the first Scripture selection for Holy Thursday is the account of the institution of the Passover in the book of Exodus (12:1-8, 11-14) and the preparation of the Passover lamb, as is explained above. A selection from Paul's First Letter to the Corinthians (11:23-26) forms the second reading. It is the account of the institution of the Eucharist and stresses the unity of the body of Christ through the breaking of the one loaf of bread and the drinking from the one cup of wine. The unique Johannine account of Jesus washing the feet of his disciples as a demonstration of love and service forms the gospel (John 13:1-15). It is through their mutual love for one another and their shared service that Christians come together for the Eucharist, that is, to celebrate the paschal mystery and paschal mystery spirituality. Then, they are sent forth to love and serve, and are called back to remember the source of their commission, and, repeating the cycle, sent forth to live paschal mystery spirituality.

The Holy Thursday celebration of the paschal mystery serves as a reminder that every Mass celebrates the paschal mystery. Preface II of the Most Holy Eucharist explains how Jesus at his last supper with his apostles established the memorial of the cross by offering himself as the unblemished lamb.[6] Furthermore, every Eucharistic Prayer, a great narrative of

---

5. Ibid., par. 16.
6. Ibid., "Order of Mass," par. 61.

praise of God for his activity throughout history, contains some reference to the paschal mystery.

For example, in Eucharistic Prayer I the priest or bishop remembers Jesus' passion, resurrection, and ascension.[7] While the reference to the paschal mystery in Eucharistic Prayer II is brief, it is, nevertheless, there as the priest or bishop remembers the Lord's death and resurrection.[8] Eucharistic Prayer III contains an elongated reference to the paschal mystery, which recalls the passion, resurrection, and ascension of God's Son.[9] However, the most detailed reference to the paschal mystery in any Eucharist Prayer is the one found in Eucharistic Prayer IV. The priest or bishop remembers Christ's death, his descent to the netherworld, his resurrection, and his ascension.[10] The recollection of the paschal mystery is followed by the offering of the body and blood of Christ under the forms of bread and wine to the Father.[11]

Eucharistic Prayer for Reconciliation I explicitly refers to the paschal mystery by naming Jesus as the new passover and remembering his death and resurrection.[12] While Eucharistic Prayer for Reconciliation II does not declare Jesus to be the new passover, it does recall his death and resurrection.[13] In the Eucharistic Prayer for Use in Masses for Various Needs I, II, III, and IV, the paschal mystery is attributed to the Father, who led Jesus through his passion, death on the cross, and resurrection.[14]

The three Eucharistic Prayers for Masses with Children each contain a reference to the paschal mystery which is simple enough for children to understand. In the first of these prayers, the priest or bishop indicates that all are doing what Jesus told them to do by remembering his death and resurrection.[15] The second of these prayers also contains the reference to

---

7. Ibid., par. 92.
8. Ibid., par. 105.
9. Ibid., par. 113.
10. Ibid., par. 122.
11. Ibid., pars. 92, 105, 113, 122.
12. Ibid., "Appendix to the Order of Mass: Eucharistic Prayers for Reconciliation I," par. 7.
13. Ibid., "Appendix to the Order of Mass: Eucharistic Prayers for Reconciliation II," par. 7.
14. Ibid., "Appendix to the Order of Mass: Eucharistic Prayer for Use in Masses for Various Needs I, II, III, IV," par. 7.
15. *Eucharistic Prayers for Masses with Children*, 7.

Jesus' death and resurrection.[16] The third prayer explicitly declares that the Eucharist is the remembrance of the paschal mystery along with the remembrance of Jesus' death and resurrection.[17]

The last aspect of the paschal mystery is the gift of the Spirit. In Eucharistic Prayers, the Holy Spirit is invoked through the outstretched hands of the priest or bishop over the bread and wine.[18] Eucharistic Prayer II asks God to send the Spirit upon the offerings so that they will become the body and blood of Christ.[19] Prayer III asks God to make holy the gifts by the Spirit.[20] And Eucharistic Prayer IV not only mentions that Jesus sent the Holy Spirit from the Father, but also asks the Father to sanctify the offerings with the same Spirit.[21]

The Eucharistic Prayers for Reconciliation I and II both ask the LORD to pour out the power of the Spirit on the offerings, [22] whereas the Eucharistic Prayer for Use in Masses for Various Needs I, II, III, and IV petitions the Father to send forth the Holy Spirit to sanctify the gifts of bread and wine so that they will become the body and blood of Christ.[23] The first Eucharistic Prayer for Masses with Children asks God the Father to send the Holy Spirit to make the gifts of bread and wine the body and blood of Jesus, his Son,[24] while the second prayer asks God the Father to send the Spirit to change the gifts of bread and wine into the body and blood of Jesus Christ.[25]

Another reference to the gift of the Holy Spirit is found after the people's acclamation, which is examined below. For example, in Prayer II, the petition is that those who share the body and blood of Christ will be gathered into one by the Holy Spirit.[26] Prayer III asks that those who are nourished by the body and blood of Christ be filled with the Holy Spirit

---

16. Ibid., 13.
17. Ibid., 19.
18. *Roman Missal*, "Order of Mass," par. 88.
19. Ibid., par. 101.
20. Ibid., par. 109.
21. Ibid., par. 117–18.
22. Ibid., "Appendix to the Order of Mass: Eucharistic Prayers for Reconciliation I, II" par. 3.
23. Ibid., "Appendix to the Order of Mass: Eucharistic Prayer for Use in Masses for Various Needs I, II, III, IV," par. 3.
24. *Eucharistic Prayers for Masses with Children*, 6.
25. Ibid., 12.
26. *Roman Missal*, "Order of Mass," par. 105.

and become one body, one spirit in Christ.[27] God is asked that the Holy Spirit may gather into one body those who partake of the body and blood of Christ in Eucharistic Prayer IV.[28]

The power of the Holy Spirit is invoked in the First Reconciliation Eucharist Prayer to gather into one body in Christ all who partake of the bread and wine.[29] Reconciliation II asks the Father to endow with his Spirit those who share the saving banquet.[30] In the Children's Eucharistic Prayers, the Father is asked to fill all present with the joy of the Spirit as they receive the body and blood of Christ,[31] to send the Spirit to all who share in the Eucharistic meal and bring them closer together,[32] and to fill with the joy of the Spirit those who receive the body and blood of Christ.[33]

Just in case the reader thinks that there still has not been enough references to the paschal mystery to connect Eucharist and Jesus' death and resurrection, most prayers, with the exception of two of those for Masses with children, contain an acclamation made by all present. After narrating Jesus' Passover supper with his apostles from the Synoptic Gospels (Mark, Matthew, Luke) in which Jesus takes bread and identifies it as his body and a cup of wine and tells his apostles that the cup of wine is his blood of the (new) covenant, the paschal mystery is recalled in one of three acclamations. Known as the mystery of faith, the first proclaims Jesus' death and resurrection, the second proclaims his death alone, and the third proclaims his cross and resurrection.[34]

Because the Eucharist is the epitome of the celebration of the paschal mystery, the "Universal Norms on the Liturgical Year and the General Roman Calendar" state, "On the first day of each week, which is known as the Day of the Lord or the Lord's Day, the church, by an apostolic tradition that

---

27. Ibid., par. 113.

28. Ibid., par. 122.

29. Ibid., "Appendix to the Order of Mass: Eucharistic Prayers for Reconciliation I," par. 7.

30. Ibid., "Appendix to the Order of Mass: Eucharistic Prayers for Reconciliation II," par. 7.

31. *Eucharistic Prayers for Masses with Children*, 8.

32. Ibid., 13.

33. Ibid., 20.

34. *Roman Missal*, "Order of Mass," pars. 91, 104,112,121; "Appendix to the Order of Mass: Eucharistic Prayers for Reconciliation I, II" par. 6; "Appendix to the Order of Mass: Eucharistic Prayer for Use in Masses for Various Needs I, II, III, IV," par. 6; *Eucharistic Prayers for Masses with Children*," 7.

draws its origin from the very day of the resurrection of Christ, celebrates the paschal mystery. Hence, Sunday must be considered the primordial feast day."[35] However, the model for the weekly commemoration of the paschal mystery is Holy Thursday.

Thus, the aspects of the paschal mystery are celebrated during every Eucharist. All five of the paschal mystery aspects—suffering, death, resurrection, ascension, and the gift of the Spirit—may not be mentioned, but some are always there in the Eucharistic Prayer.

REFLECTION

Eucharist or the Lord's Supper is celebrated in churches, in pizza restaurants, and in cafeterias in various degrees of solemnity. Any meal with another or others is an act of sharing food. "Pass the potatoes" means to pass and share self with others. Special meals—weddings, funerals, Easter, Christmas, etc.—renew family ties. Attendees tell stories of suffering (surgery, mishaps, accidents), death (old age, submission, lifestyle change), resurrection (moving, healing, exercising), ascension (acceptance, perspective, results), and Spirit (found in community, games, entertainment). All who share a meal are bonded together as one.

Eucharist is supposed to do the same. Those who remember the paschal mystery of Jesus discover that what happened to Jesus is happening to them. Their paschal mystery spirituality sends them from the celebration to engage in charity, signified by washing feet during the Holy Thursday liturgy. Washing feet is nothing other than dying before another in service to him or her. Maybe washing the body of an elderly person better communicates the significance of Holy Thursday's act of taking a basin of water and washing another person's feet. Likewise, the action of making a blanket or quilt and giving it to the homeless is just like washing feet. Serving food in a soup kitchen is another way we wash feet. Paschal mystery spirituality is living daily what is celebrated once a year on Holy Thursday and every Sunday. All experiences of feet washing are brought together into one, and then all marking Holy Thursday and every Sunday are sent out as one to spread the charity of paschal mystery spirituality everywhere.

1. How does the Hebrew Passover serve as a matrix for interpreting Jesus' suffering, death, resurrection, ascension, and gift of the Spirit?

---

35. Ibid., "Universal Norms," par. 4.

1. How does the Hebrew Passover serve as a matrix for interpreting events of your life?
2. Why is it important to remember the aspects of Jesus' paschal mystery in every Eucharist? Why is it important to remember the aspects of your paschal mystery in every Eucharist?
3. If you become what you eat, what do you become after celebrating the paschal mystery using bread and wine?
4. What is the role of the Holy Spirit in the celebration of Eucharist? What is the role of the Holy Spirit in your life?
5. How does each aspect of the paschal mystery of Jesus fit into your paschal mystery spirituality?

8

Friday of the Passion of the Lord: Part 1

THERE CAN BE NO doubt that the focus of Good Friday is the paschal mystery. The Good Friday service is titled "The Celebration of the Passion of the Lord."[1] The first choice for the opening Prayer states that by shedding his blood, Christ established the paschal mystery.[2] The second choice for the opening Prayer declares that he abolished death.[3]

The first Scripture selection is the Fourth Song of the Servant of Yahweh. The references to the servant's suffering are, obviously, applied to the suffering and death of Jesus. The author writes:

> He was despised and rejected by others; a man of suffering and acquainted with infirmity. . . . Surely he has borne our infirmities and carried our diseases; yet we accounted him stricken, struck down by God, and afflicted. But he was wounded for our transgressions, crushed for our iniquities; upon him was the punishment that made us whole, and by his bruises we are healed. He was

---

1. *Roman Missal*, 314.
2. Ibid., "Friday of the Passion of the Lord [Good Friday]," par. 6.
3. Ibid.

oppressed, and he was afflicted, yet he did not open his mouth; like a lamb that is led to the slaughter, and like a sheep that before its shearers is silent, so he did not open his mouth. (Isa 53:3a, 4–5, 7).

The response to this reading is taken from Psalm 31. Appropriately, verse 12 is sung: "I have passed out of mind like one who is dead; I have become like a broken vessel" (Ps 31:12). Just as the passage from Isaiah is applied to Jesus' suffering, the psalm, using the metaphor of a broken dish that is tossed into the trash and forgotten is also applied to Jesus and used to interpret his death.

The second reading on Good Friday is taken from the Letter to the Hebrews. This selection employs two of the major themes surrounding suffering in Hebrews. The first focuses on Jesus, the great high priest, who understood the weakness of humanity. The author of Hebrews writes, " . . . [W]e do not have a high priest who is unable to sympathize with our weaknesses, but we have one who in every respect has been tested as we are . . . " (Heb 4:15). The second focus is on the obedience which Jesus learned through his suffering and how it perfected him. Hebrews records, "Although he was a Son, he learned obedience through what he suffered; and having been made perfect, he became the source of eternal salvation for all who obey him" (Heb 5:8–9).

Hebrews focuses on the priesthood and sacrifice of Jesus, using Hebrew Bible (Old Testament) images to illustrate Christian Bible (New Testament) fulfillment. Suffering is treated in a number of passages, all of which indicate that it is to be looked upon as a discipline. The anonymous author declares that Jesus is the mediator of a new covenant (Heb 12:24), which is the result of his suffering and death on the cross. " . . . [F]or the sake of the joy that was set before him," the author writes, he "endured the cross, disregarding its shame, and has taken his seat at the right hand of the throne of God" (Heb 12:2). Through his paschal mystery, he has become "the pioneer and perfecter of . . . faith" (Heb 12:2).

Earlier in the work, the author expresses the same ideas by writing, " . . . [W]e do see Jesus . . . now crowned with glory and honor because of the suffering of death, so that by the grace of God he might taste death for everyone" (Heb 2:9). Through Jesus' suffering and death, he has consecrated people by his own blood (Heb 13:12) and established a new covenant.

Hebrews makes it clear that Jesus was tested through what he suffered and is able to understand human weakness: "Because he himself was tested by what he suffered, he is able to help those who are being tested" (Heb

2:18). In other words, Jesus' suffering was a discipline which strengthened him and enabled him to be the priest and the sacrifice offered to God. Furthermore, having passed the test of suffering, he serves as a model of how to suffer for his followers. According to the author of Hebrews, suffering made Jesus perfect. The author states that it is fitting that God, "for whom and through whom all things exist, . . . should make the pioneer of . . . salvation perfect through sufferings" (Heb 2:10). This suffering, which was once for all (Heb 9:25–28), is held up as an example for the followers of Jesus. If they learn discipline from suffering, they will be made perfect. Nowhere is this expressed more clearly than in chapter 12 of Hebrews (12:7, 9–10).

There is no doubt that disciplined suffering is painful, but it brings the peaceful fruit of righteousness to those who are trained by it (Heb 12:11). Therefore, followers of Jesus should endure the great contest of suffering (Heb 10:32) and even join in the sufferings of those in prison and joyfully accept the confiscation of property, knowing that they have a better and lasting possession (Heb 10:34). The author reminds his readers that they need endurance to do the will of God and to receive what he has promised (Heb 10:36). Followers of Jesus need disciplined suffering to live paschal mystery spirituality.

REFLECTION

Suffering requires discipline. We learn disciplined obedience from our suffering. By giving of ourselves—sacrificing ourselves in some manner—we practice the type of discipline which the author of Hebrews writes about. By facing the rough and toughest parts of daily life instead of procrastinating or trying to dodge them, we are trained in the discipline of suffering. Suffering tests our wills. Its rigors enable us to endure.

Our place of work requires discipline in order to face our tasks and get them accomplished. An author knows that writing is disciplined suffering; he or she must sit down and get his or her hands on the keyboard. An automobile mechanic must get his hands on the engine and take it apart and put it back together. Fixing the car is a discipline; it involves suffering. Likewise, the person who works on the assembly line must impose discipline on himself or herself in order to keep up with the speed of the line and put together whatever it is that his or her company manufactures. Even daily chores, like loading and unloading the dishwasher, dusting the house, washing the windows, etc., involve some suffering.

We suffer when we keep a promise. If you tell your children that you will take them to a movie which you do not want to see, you suffer when you discipline yourself to keep your promise. If you hate going shopping at the mall, then you suffer when you discipline yourself to go there and take care of your need to buy some new clothes or new shoes. Another person may speak to you about a personal problem and ask that you promise not to tell another. Disciplined suffering is involved in keeping your lips sealed.

Keeping ourselves healthy involves disciplined suffering. A diet is important, but it is not easy to always eat the right kinds of foods. In fact, we discipline ourselves to suffer through a program of weight loss, when we discover that we have eaten too much. Ask anyone who has quit smoking or cut down on alcohol and he or she will share with you his or her suffering caused by discipline.

Exercise involves suffering. In the midst of an already crowded day, exercise must be scheduled. This means that we suffer from the loss of the free time we have to give up in order to suffer at the health club! Many people face the prospect of exercise with dread because it requires disciplined suffering. Jogging, bicycling, swimming, or any other type of aerobic exercise is a discipline with suffering which must be endured.

Like children who are disciplined by their parents, suffering is for our own good. A parent may punish a child by grounding him or her or sending him or her to his or her room. Sometimes the child must clean up his or her room. Other times, the child is made to sit at his or her desk and finish homework from school. Why do parents do these things to their children? They love them and want them to learn the art of disciplined suffering.

Disciplined suffering makes us better people. Through it, our wills are strengthened to face life and to live it fully. The example of one who engaged in disciplined suffering is Jesus. He sympathized with our weakness. This means that he was one in harmony with all that is human—including our inability to always discipline ourselves to suffer. Through his passion—suffering and cross—he demonstrated how to face suffering in a disciplined manner. Discipleship, according to Hebrews, is learning disciplined obedience from our suffering, like Jesus. Paschal mystery spirituality is living a life of discipline.

1. What has been your most recent experience of suffering which functioned as discipline for you?

2. Identify three ways in which your disciplined suffering has made you a better person. How has that disciplined suffering taught you obedience to God? How has that disciplined suffering made you perfect?

3. What suffering have you endured which has enabled you to be sympathetic to others' suffering? Explain.

4. When have you most recently had to impose suffering on another in order to discipline that person?

5. What are your thoughts and feelings about the principal theme—suffering is discipline—found in the Letter to the Hebrews?

6. How does disciplined suffering fit into your paschal mystery spirituality?

9

Friday of the Passion of the Lord:
Part 2

THE GOSPEL FOR GOOD Friday is the passion according to John (John 18:1—19:42). Besides the reference to Jesus as the new passover lamb, as explained above, John's Gospel is not interested in portraying Jesus as one who suffers. Thus, there is a definite contrast between the focus on suffering in the passage from the Letter to the Hebrews and John's Gospel! There are no predictions concerning Jesus' passion in this gospel. He speaks of going away (John 13:33), but the reference is to his glorification, which has already taken place (John 13:31–32).

In this gospel, written around 100 CE, Jesus is consistently portrayed as being in charge of his passion and death. After setting the stage for Jesus' arrest, the author of the Fourth Gospel informs his readers that " . . . Jesus, knowing all that was to happen to him," came out of the garden to meet his betrayer (John 18:4). In this scenario, it is important to notice that Jesus, the accused, asks all of the questions: "Whom are you looking for?" (John 18:4, 7). When they reply, "Jesus of Nazareth," Jesus says to them, "I am he" (John 18:5), and "they stepped back and fell to the ground" (John 18:6). In other words, according to John, Jesus' accusers fall down and worship him, when he names himself God by using the LORD's own self-designation of I AM (Exodus 3:14).

When Jesus is questioned by Annas, he counters his questions with his own (John 18:19–24). Likewise, when Pilate tries him, Jesus seems to have the upper hand. Pilate is portrayed as one who does not want to have Jesus put to death, but is forced into it by politics (John 18:28—19:16).

In John's Gospel, Jesus carries the cross himself (John 19:17). He entrusts the care of his mother to the unnamed disciple whom he loved (John 19:26) and the care of the disciple to his mother (John 19:25–27). His final words are those of accomplishment. He says, "It is finished" (John 19:30). The "it" refers to doing "the will of him who sent" Jesus (John 4:34; 5:30, 36; 6:38; 9:4; 10:18; 17:4). Doing the Father's will means suffering, death, and resurrection, which are referred to in John's Gospel as glorification, Jesus' hour, and exaltation. If the unique story of the wedding at Cana (John 2:1–11) is considered one bookend of John's Gospel, and the unique story of wine put on hyssop and held to Jesus' mouth (John 19:28-30) is the other bookend, then the "it" of "It is finished" (John 19:30a) can refer to Jesus' completion of his mission, namely, the union of people (bride) and God (groom). In completing his mission, Jesus is glorified, his hour arrives, and he is exalted.

First, glorification: In his dialogue with Nicodemus, Jesus says, " . . . [J]ust as Moses lifted up the serpent in the wilderness, so must the Son of Man be lifted up" (John 3:14). After his entry into Jerusalem, Jesus tells a crowd, " . . . [W]hen I am lifted up from the earth, [I] will draw all people to myself" (John 12:32). The author adds this comment: "He said this to indicate the kind of death he was to die" (John 12:33). In the trial scene before Pilate, the author writes that the Jews tell Pilate, "We are not permitted to put anyone to death," and the author informs the reader that they said this in order " . . . to fulfill what Jesus had said when he indicated the kind of death he was to die" (John 18:31–32).

Second, hour: The Johannine Jesus is in control of his death, which is also his exaltation. He refers to it as his hour. At the wedding at Cana, after Jesus' mother points out to him that they have run out of wine, he replies, "My hour has not yet come" (John 2:4b). The same phrase is echoed after Jesus finishes teaching in the temple area and upsets the authorities. The author of this gospel records, " . . . [T]hey tried to arrest him, but no one laid hands on him, because his hour had not yet come" (John 7:30). Again, after Jesus teaches that he is the light of the world, John writes, "He spoke these words while teaching in the treasury of the temple, but no one arrested him, because his hour had not yet come" (John 8:20).

After Jesus makes his entry into Jerusalem, however, his hour does come. John portrays him as telling his disciples, "The hour has come for the Son of Man to be glorified" (John 12:23). This will be accomplished through his suffering and death on the cross—his paschal mystery. Because he is all-knowing, the Johannine Jesus says, "Now my soul is troubled. And what should I say—'Father, save me from this hour'? No, it is for this reason that I have come to this hour" (John 12:27).

Before Jesus begins to wash the feet of his disciples, the author of this gospel prepares the reader for the joining together of Passover and Jesus' death. He writes, "Now before the festival of the Passover, Jesus knew that his hour had come to depart from this world and go to the Father" (John 13:1). Employing a metaphor which is more typical of the Synoptic authors' portrayal of Jesus' agony in the garden of Gethsemane, after his arrest Jesus asks Peter, "Am I not to drink the cup that the Father has given me?" (John 18:11b) Thus, in John's Gospel, not only is Passover reinterpreted in light of Jesus, but drinking the cup becomes the means to his exaltation.

Third, exaltation: Thus, in this gospel, the hour of Jesus' death simultaneously is also the moment of his exaltation, for when he is lifted up on the cross and slaughtered like a paschal lamb, he passes over from death to life. The author of the Fourth Gospel ties together the account of the institution of the Passover, which is found in the book of Exodus (12:1–28), the prophet Isaiah's comparison of the suffering servant to a "lamb that is led to the slaughter" (Isa 53:7), and the possible allusion to the triumphant, apocalyptic lamb found in the Book of Revelation (5:6—7:17; 17:14; 19:7; 21:9, 14, 22).

Throughout his gospel, John predicts that Judas will hand over Jesus to the authorities. After the discourse on the bread of life, Jesus asks the Twelve, "Did I not choose you, the twelve? Yet one of you is a devil" (John 6:70). Then, the author informs the reader, "He was speaking of Judas son of Simon Iscariot; for he, though one of the twelve, was going to betray him" (John 6:71). After Mary anoints Jesus' feet in Bethany, the author again makes an editorial comment about "Judas Iscariot, one of his disciples (the one who was about to betray him)" (John 12:4).

Before Jesus washes the feet of his disciples, the author informs the reader, "The devil had already put it into the heart of Judas son of Simon

Iscariot to betray [Jesus]" (John 13:2). This event has been forecast several times; Judas' culpability is lessened because the devil is blamed for Judas' action. After the disciples' feet are washed and Jesus explains his action, the Johannine Jesus then says, " . . . One of you will betray me" (John 13:21). One disciple asks, "Lord, who is it?" and Jesus answers, "It is the one to whom I give this piece of bread when I have dipped it in the dish" (John 13:25–26). This editorial comment follows: "So when he had dipped the piece of bread, he gave it to Judas son of Simon Iscariot. After he received the piece of bread, Satan entered into him. Jesus said to him, 'Do quickly what you are going to do.' So, after receiving the piece of bread, he immediately went out" (John 13:26–27, 30).

It comes as no surprise to the reader when Jesus enters a garden and the author writes, " . . . Judas, who betrayed him, also knew the place, because Jesus often met there with his disciples. So Judas brought a detachment of soldiers together with police from the chief priests and the Pharisees, and came there with lanterns and torches and weapons" (John 18:2–3). John records no betraying kiss. In fact, after this last mention of Judas, he disappears from John's Gospel. The author is not interested in making a statement about Judas' act, but he must record it in order to be faithful to the tradition which remembered him as betraying Jesus. All that John seems to hint at is that Judas' betrayal was somehow fore-ordained. Even though Judas hands him over, Jesus is, nevertheless, in charge of what happens.

This is also true in the case of Peter's betrayal. After the Johannine Jesus explains to his disciples that he will be with them only a little while longer (John 13:33), Peter says to Jesus that he will lay down his life for him (John 13:37). Jesus answers him, "Will you lay down your life for me? . . . I tell you, before the cock crows, you will have denied me three times" (John 13:38). Jesus' prediction is fulfilled. After he is arrested, Peter follows Jesus to the gate outside the courtyard of the high priest. When the maid asks Peter if he is one of Jesus' disciples, he declares that he is not one of them (John 18:17). When the guards, and then one of the slaves, ask Peter the same question, he again states that he is not one of Jesus' disciples. And immediately the cock crows (John 18:25–27).

John's Gospel records no conversion on Peter's part. Rather, the author of this gospel rehabilitates Peter by not only presenting him as one of the first witnesses to the empty tomb (John 20:1–10), but by uniquely portraying him as confessing his love for Jesus three times (John 21:15–17). Peter's three-fold confession of love and Jesus' three-fold commission serves to counteract his earlier three-fold denial.

REFLECTION

In John's Gospel, passion—suffering and death—is triumphant! Obviously, that statement is paradoxical; it seems to be contradictory, but upon closer examination we begin to realize that it is filled with truth. At the very moment of his death, the Johannine Jesus is lifted up; he is exalted. In order to achieve such a narrative paradox, the author of John's Gospel must portray Jesus as being in charge of everything. Not only does this make him God and the Son of God, but it also removes all culpability for his death from the characters named Pilate, Peter, and Judas. The crucifixion of Jesus is, simultaneously, his hour of glorification and exaltation in the Fourth Gospel.

What is true for the Johannine Jesus is also true for us. Sometimes the moment of our suffering and metaphorical death is the moment of our triumph. This is a deep truth, but it needs exploration. For example, the birth of a child is simultaneously a time of suffering for his or her mother and father and a time of joy for the parents who have waited for nine months for this exact moment. Taking care of the child will bring even more suffering—sleepless nights, waiting to see doctors, maybe surgery—for the parents. Yet, their love for each other and their child leads them triumphantly onward! One day in the distant future they will experience even more triumph when their child enters high school, gets his or her driver's license, graduates from high school, and heads off to college.

Authentic human relationships are filled with the paradox that passion is triumph. A lot of suffering occurs through human relating. We often disagree with each other. We often determine what the other needs to do without any consideration as to who the other person really is. And presupposition lights many fires that would never have been started if a simple question were asked. When two people enter into a dialogical relationship, revealing themselves to each other, suffering—through hours of clarifying dialogue—and death—through turning lose of power and presupposition—bring moments of triumphant love that is so palpable that it can be touched. For this to be experienced, each person in the relationship has to suffer and die in order for mutual love to triumph.

Even working on a team of any kind is filled with the paradox of suffering and death leading to triumph. A team of people represents a single focus by a group of individuals, who, if they want to accomplish whatever project they are facing, have to die to their individuality and rise to their status as one, unified team. This is very difficult to do in a culture that glamorizes the individual. We see this in sports with hot shots, who are out to show off their skills instead of use them for the good of the team. We see this in offices, where getting ahead, getting a raise, getting a promotion take first place to giving the team its due. Even in churches, those who are supposed to form the body of Christ challenge the whole by threatening to disappear if they don't get their way, their music, or their representatives on boards or councils. Triumph is had only when all the members of the team die to themselves and submit themselves to the greater common good instead of focusing on what is good for the individual.

Weller says that United States culture displays "a compulsive avoidance of difficult matters and an obsession with distraction."[1] He states that the depths of truth are often divided in an ascension culture. "We love rising, and we fear going down," states Weller. "Consequently, we find ways to deny the reality of this rich but difficult territory, and we are thinned psychically."[2] Good Friday offers people the opportunity to descend into the dark of Jesus' death and, simultaneously, spiritually descend into the dark of their own future death. In other words, they can participate in death and resurrection.

The truth that John's Gospel presents on Good Friday of the Passion of the Lord is that suffering and death are triumphant! Jesus lived that paradox, that seemingly contradictory statement. He not only lived it, he demonstrated it through his own suffering and death on a cross. The very moment of his death was also the very moment of his being lifted up, his exaltation. Thus, the crucifixion of Jesus in John's Gospel is, simultaneously, his hour of glorification and exaltation—a deep truth if ever there was one! And that truth is discovered in paschal mystery spirituality.

1. How has your suffering and death been paradoxical?
2. Like the Johannine Jesus, what cross have you carried alone?
3. How have you experienced God's glory through suffering?
4. How have you experienced the hour (or a few minutes) of Jesus' exaltation?

1. Weller, "Geography of Sorrow," 5.
2. Ibid.

5. Who has been a Judas in your life? Was that experience a test? Was that experience the unfolding of God's plan for you? Explain.

6. Are you more like the Johannine Judas or Peter? Explain.

7. What are your thoughts and feelings about the principal theme—suffering and death are simultaneously triumph—found in John's Gospel?

8. How does triumphant suffering and death fit into your paschal mystery spirituality?

10

Friday of the Passion of the Lord: Part 3

AFTER THE PROCLAMATION OF the Scripture texts assigned to Good Friday, the priest or bishop gives a short homily,[1] then he begins The Solemn Intercessions.[2] The ten intercessions specifically pray for the whole church, the pope, all orders of the faithful, catechumens, Christian unity, Jewish people, those who do not believe in Christ, those who do not believe in God, those in public office, and those in tribulation of any kind. Then, following the intercessions is the adoration of the cross.[3]

The priest or bishop presents a wooden cross, not a crucifix with an image of the crucified Jesus on it, to the congregants declaring that on the wood of the cross hung the salvation of the world.[4] Members of the assembly then approach the cross to genuflect before it, to kiss it, or to touch

---

1. *Roman Missal*, "Friday of the Passion of the Lord [Good Friday]," par. 10.
2. Ibid., pars. 11–13.
3. Ibid., par. 14.
4. Ibid., par. 15.

it.⁵ This gesture is meant to get people in touch, literally and figuratively, with Jesus' paschal mystery and their own paschal mystery spirituality. As indicated above, the cross, which Jesus carries alone in John's Gospel, is, simultaneously, the instrument of death and resurrection (glorification, being lifted up).

Genuflecting before the cross, kissing it, or touching it is meant to remind people that disciplined suffering is transformative; disciplined suffering changes people, hopefully conforming them more and more into paschal mystery spirituality. The Johannine Jesus demonstrates how to reach out and grasp the pain in order to let it transform him, rather than spending all energy attempting to avoid it or passing it on to others. He destroys death not by cancelling it, but by passing through it and making the cross a trophy of victory over it. Through Jesus, God transforms all things.

One of the best images of transformation is found in the Christian Bible (New Testament) Book of Revelation. When John of Patmos describes his heavenly throne room vision, he sees "a Lamb standing as if it had been slaughtered" (Rev 5:6). The slaughtered paschal lamb from the Hebrew Bible (Old Testament) Book of Exodus has become the transformed or resurrected Lamb in the Christian Bible (New Testament) Book of Revelation. Jesus' suffering and death, as presented by the Book of Revelation in iconic form, have transformed him into a higher state or risen life. By living paschal mystery spirituality, people draw upon the Lamb's power to transform them.

The Johannine Jesus also demonstrates that God suffers with people. If Jesus, the Word, who was with God and was God (John 1:1) participated in suffering and death on the cross, then God is not just watching suffering and death, but participating in it through Christ his Son. The Johannine Jesus did not merely observe suffering from afar, but he inhabited it as a human being. Yes, any type of suffering is unjust and undeserved, but it is the result of being human. He, who is God, used tragedy, suffering, pain, betrayal, and death on a cross in order to reveal that God suffers with people. In other words, Jesus revealed God's presence in the paschal mystery through the aspects of suffering and death. Indeed, suffering and death may be the only thing strong enough to conquer the self that continues to rail against the very aspects God uses to draw all into paschal mystery spirituality.

---

5. Ibid., par. 18.

Because sacraments are not celebrated on Good Friday,[6] after the veneration of the cross, the instrument which brought about the paschal mystery, a communion service is celebrated with Eucharistic bread kept from Holy Thursday's Mass of the Lord's Supper. The Prayer after Communion re-emphasizes the paschal mystery by mentioning Christ's death and resurrection, as does the Prayer over the People.[7] Thus, Good Friday's celebration of the Lord's passion, his suffering and death as a passover lamb, is concluded in the same way in which it began—by referencing the paschal mystery.

REFLECTION

Our first response to suffering is to avoid the pain even though we may know that it can transform us. It is easier to blame someone else because that, seemingly, gives us power over suffering. We can also flee from it. We can deny it. We can find many ways not to have to engage in the inner work of honest self-knowledge that is essential to embrace the transformation that is the result of living paschal mystery spirituality. However, we come face-to-face with the cross on Good Friday, and it reminds us that surrender is required for anyone who follows Jesus.

The First Letter of Peter presents Jesus as a model for good Christian suffering and death. When the pattern is traced in the Christian, it can give him or her hope. The author writes that the prophets confirm that good suffering leads to future glory (1 Pet 1:10–11). He states that Christ suffered in order to lead people to God (1 Pet 3:18). In fact, when Jesus "was abused, he did not return abuse; when he suffered, he did not threaten; but he entrusted himself to the one who judges justly" (1 Pet 2:23). Therefore, using paradox, First Peter declares that by Jesus' wounds people have been healed (1 Pet 2:24b).

Therefore, whenever anyone bears the pain of unjust suffering, he or she experiences grace. Furthermore, whenever anyone bears the pain of just suffering, that is, doing what is right, he or she can be assured of God's approval. Indeed, "[i]t is better to suffer for doing good, if suffering should be God's will, than to suffer for doing evil" (1 Pet 3:17). Again, the example is Christ's suffering; he left an example for all to follow in his footsteps (1 Pet 2:19–21). Consolation can be found in the fact that fellow believers

---

6. Ibid., par. 1.
7. Ibid., pars. 30–31.

throughout the world are undergoing the same types of sufferings (1 Pet 5:9). After suffering for a little while, the God of all grace, who has called one to his eternal glory in Christ, will himself restore, confirm, strengthen, and establish one (1 Pet 5:10).

Christians, therefore, should rejoice to the extent that they share in the sufferings of Christ, so that when his glory is revealed they may also rejoice exultantly (1 Pet 4:13). They should not be ashamed to suffer; rather, they should glorify God because they bear his name (1 Pet 4:16). Through suffering, according to the First Letter of Peter, a Christian is conformed to the pattern of Jesus. Just as Jesus suffered, so the Christian suffers. This suffering is one's hope that he or she will share in the same glory which Christ now shares—because of his or her suffering. Therefore, the Christian should always be ready to give an explanation to anyone who asks for a reason for hope (1 Pet 3:15).

First Peter's good suffering is reflected in Buber's spirituality. Kramer presents "[t]wo interrelated elements of Buber's dialogical spirituality" that "concretely embody aspects of dying before dying."[8] The first is the practice of turning away from self-interests and individually oriented preoccupations in order to turn toward God.[9] That is, genuine turning flows from dying to oneself, states Kramer.[10] It involves revising one's normal direction of movement, forgetting one's separate self, and un-self-consciously engaging, addressing, and responding to the other.[11]

The second element of dying is "opening up and letting go" of whatever one is holding onto.[12] Such receptivity implies authentic surrender, letting go of control, and suspending all self-conscious reflection. We become more alive, present, and open to interacting with others. According to Kramer, "[t]urning toward and surrendering into teaches us the art of letting go of the need to be in control of our lives."[13] Through practice, this spiritual dying facilitates "a death/rebirth through which attachments to the self-reflexive, isolated ego again and again naturally and spontaneously dissolve through turning toward and surrendering into genuine encounters."[14]

---

8. Kramer, *Martin Buber's Spirituality*, 101.
9. Ibid.
10. Ibid.
11. Ibid.
12. Ibid., 102.
13. Ibid.
14. Ibid.

And it is not just surrender that is among the requirements for good suffering or dying before dying; it is also practicing dying. Meditation or reflection can be the vehicle to let go or loose our attachment to our illusion of control of our lives. We can liberate ourselves, like Jesus did, by dying into silence, dying to the past, dying to the future, and completely letting go, declaring that for the moment our mission is finished. Learning how to die gracefully is simultaneously learning how to trust that God transforms suffering and death into life.

Kramer notes that another way to practice dying before dying can occur when one surrenders fully into relationship with God in prayer.[15] Kramer also says that dying can occur when we let go of our need to look good and to be right.[16] Those ways of practicing dying—and many more—represent how one hallows death, according to Kramer.[17] For Buber hallowing death means "bringing an attitude of reverence into everything that we encounter, relating to everything as holy."[18] Thus, "hallowing death involves bringing the awareness of dying into the holiness of every moment. . . . Whenever we turn fully and surrender totally to what we encounter without holding anything back, without trying to possess it, we pass through a mini-death experience."[19] Furthermore, "hallowing death means holding/discovering/relating to death with an attitude of reverence and remaining open to its holiness by recognizing God's presence in its midst."[20]

The adoration of the cross on Good Friday becomes an invitation to look deeper into the death of Jesus and discover the need for our own suffering and dying. It is, of course, helpful to realize we cannot ever die because we participate in what is eternal through the paschal mystery. There are numerous times when we must let go of how we think life must be and surrender to God. Opportunities for surrender, suffering, are opportunities for dying. These deaths enable us to learn how to choose transformation. These little deaths are practice sessions for final death. Indeed, if we participate in paschal mystery spirituality now, we know the truth of transformation and are able to embrace it over and over again. Transformation is the result of emptying (death). Transcendence is the result of transformation.

15. Ibid., 103.
16. Ibid.
17. Ibid., 99.
18. Ibid., 100.
19. Ibid.
20. Ibid.

The ritual of adoring the cross is meant to take people out of their "familiar mode of functioning and into an altered state of consciousness."[21] According to Weller, ritual "has the capacity to derange [people], to shake [them] out of the old forms."[22] Ritual is meant to remind them that everyone and everything they love, they will lose. That is a harsh truth, but it is paschal mystery truth. Those who spend their lives denying death so readily cannot continue to do so on Good Friday when they come forward to adore the cross, the instrument of Jesus' death. Even if it is only for a moment, people are transformed. They are "supposed to emerge from a ritual wondering what the hell just happened," states Weller.[23] "Ritual connects [them] to spirit and soul. It can shift [them] out of [their] usual state of mind."[24]

Jenkinson notes "that most dying people spend their time *not* dying."[25] Jenkinson argues that in North American culture people do not know how to die because they do not know how to live in relationship with others. "This pseudoculture is founded on the idea of self-sufficiency, self-determinism, and the sanctity of the individual," states Jenkinson.[26] Living on a farm, Jenkinson says, "the connection between death and life is clear, but in most of the culture a deep understanding of death doesn't enter into people's choices or their manner of life. . . ."[27]

Jenkinson says that the reason North American culture denies death is because it practices no ending rituals. He has in mind rituals that, for instance, kill off adolescence through isolation, fasting, and darkness, and initiate the adolescent into "her or his personal, meaning-burdened death in a ritual guided by older people whose lives have prepared them for such moments."[28] Such initiation into adulthood, according to Jenkinson, enables one "to see the centrality of death in life, which is the beginning of [one's] capacity to participate deeply in the indebtedness that is the basis of all real culture."[29]

---

21. Weller, "Geography of Sorrow," 7.
22. Ibid., 13.
23. Ibid.
24. Ibid.
25. Jenkinson, "As We Lay Dying," 6.
26. Ibid., 7.
27. Ibid., 10.
28. Ibid., 11.
29. Ibid.

This is what the adoration of the cross is designed to do. It brings those attending the Good Friday service face to face with Jesus' death and, simultaneously, their own death. Jenkinson says that death doesn't burden life; it animates life. "The centrality of death gives [one] a chance to live, because it says, 'Here's the bad news; it's not going to last. And here's the good news: it's not going to last.'"[30] According to Jenkinson, "The news of [one's] imminent demise is enabling, when all is said and done."[31] Furthermore, the adoration of the cross reminds people not to spend their time "*not* dying, refusing to let their death become something nutritious that could feed the world that had sustained them."[32] Adoring the cross is supposed to be a transformational experience through death to new life.

Vinzent describes Meister Eckhart's understanding of the Eucharist as "our transformation into God and of God into us."[33] Vinzent writes: "What is being transformed always takes on the complete being—matter and form—of that into which it is being transformed. Transformation into God means that we are entirely what God is; God's transformation into our creaturely being of multiplicity and multitude is his changing entirely into the plurality."[34] Eating the body of Christ and drinking his blood converts us into God—because Jesus Christ is God—and God converts himself into us.[35] Every time we celebrate the Eucharist, according to Eckhart, we are transformed into God, and God is transformed into us. This is the mystery of paschal mystery spirituality. It is also why the cross—the instrument that transformed Jesus from death to life—is adored on Good Friday before communion is shared.

When writing about the Christian Bible (New Testament) letters of Paul and his use of the cross as the instrument of Jesus' death, Carolyn Osiek brings out the oxymoron contained in the apostle's writings:

> When Paul speaks of the word of the cross that he was sent to preach, he realizes that for most residents of the Roman world, especially those not in places of power, the very symbol of the cross was all too familiar as an instrument of execution. It provoked terror of violence, cruelty, and death. The "power of the cross" is

30. Ibid.
31. Ibid., 12.
32. Ibid., 13.
33. Vinzent, "Neither Money nor Delights," 119.
34. Ibid.
35. Ibid.

an oxymoron, the juxtaposition of two words that simply do not go together. Yet for Paul they very much did go together. Precisely what is otherwise understood to be abject weakness, defeat, and shame becomes the source of power for those who believe through the death and rising of Christ (1 Cor 1:17–18). Even though his blunt language of cross and crucifixion must have been jolting and even repulsive to some, he boldly throws it out, leaving it to the hearer to wrestle with it.[36]

Because we live in a death-denying culture, not only does it become imperative that we wrestle with Jesus' death on the cross, but that we wrestle also with our own death. Understanding paschal mystery spirituality helps us to grasp the truth that nothing ever has to die permanently. Even some scientists now proclaim that nothing dies! It is all transformed. By dying we come to know exactly what life is. Again, oxymoronically, death is the doorway to life! But if we keep seeking ways to deny death its place in our lives, then we are also denying God's power to raise life out of death. Thus, resurrection is happening all the time for those who trust God.

Good Friday invites us to look deeper into the pattern of suffering, death, and rising in our human lives now. Good Friday is an invitation to participate in the eternal dying and rising of Christ, which Jesus instituted through his paschal mystery. While all great religions of the world talk about suffering, death, and new life, Jesus actually participated in them. Through his paschal mystery, he changes our minds about God, who is more interested in participating in them with us and leading us through them than letting us experience them alone.

Thus, dying has become a holy event. In the "Masses and Prayers for Various Needs and Occasions" in *The Roman Missal*, there is a Mass for the Dying. In the Collect, the priest or bishop reminds God that it was through death that he has opened the gate to eternal life. Then, he prays for the dying person who is united to Jesus' passion in his or her final struggle.[37] Likewise, in the Prayer after Communion, at the hour of death we pray that the dying be able to pass over from this life to eternal life.[38] In the Prayer over the Offerings in the Mass for the Grace of a Happy Death, the pray-ers are reminded that God has destroyed death by the death of his Son, and that by obeying God's will even until death all may be made shar-

---

36. Osiek, "Power of the Cross," 213–14.
37. *Roman Missal*, 1315.
38. Ibid., 1316.

ers in Christ's resurrection.[39] Likewise, in the Prayer after Communion for the same Mass, the Eucharist is described as the pledge of immortality so that at the moment all depart in death they may be restored to life through Christ.[40]

1. How is the cross an image of death and new life for you?
2. How has your disciplined suffering transformed you?
3. How have you experienced the cross as a trophy of victory?
4. How have you experienced God suffering with you?
5. When have you experienced good, patient suffering?
6. What experience has been dying before dying for you?
7. How do you hallow death?
8. How has the cross been an oxymoron for you?
9. How is dying a holy event?
10. How does dying fit into your paschal mystery spirituality?

---

39. Ibid., 1317.
40. Ibid., 1318.

11

The Easter Vigil in the Holy Night

THE EASTER VIGIL ON Holy Saturday evening[1] continues to focus on the paschal mystery by comparing the Passover which celebrated the exodus for the Israelites to the passover which celebrates the exodus of Jesus from the tomb of death to the realm of resurrection. The first words of instruction by the priest or bishop mention that this paschal solemnity is the sacred night when the Lord Jesus Christ passed over from death to life.[2] "The Easter Proclamation" (Exsultet) also emphasizes the connection between the previous Passover event and the new passover event. The deacon sings about the feasts of passover, celebrating the one true Lamb's (Jesus') slaughter and how his blood anoints the doorposts of believers. He broke the prison-bars of death and rose victorious from the underworld. In fact, the first Passover and the second passover are declared to be occurring again this night. God is again freeing his people from slavery and enabling them to pass dry-shod

---

1. *Roman Missal*, "Easter Sunday of the Resurrection of the Lord: The Easter Vigil in the Holy Night," par. 3.

2. Ibid., par. 9.

through the Red Sea. This night the pillar of fire, represented by the paschal candle, which is a sign of the risen Christ, leads the way.[3]

Nine Scripture texts are assigned to the Easter Vigil. Of these, four focus directly on the paschal mystery, while the other five recalls how God saved his people throughout history and, now saves them through the paschal work of his own Son.[4]

The second reading (Gen 22:1–18) narrates Abraham's willingness to take his son, Isaac, to the land of Moriah, where he would offer him as a holocaust on a height (Gen 22:2). Because of Abraham's faithfulness in obeying God, the Lord's messenger stays his hand and Isaac passes over from imminent death to life. However, Abraham spies a ram caught by its horns in a thicket, so he takes the ram and offers it as a holocaust in place of his son (Gen 22:13). It is not difficult to make the connection between Abraham's only son, who was spared from death, and God's only Son, Jesus, who was slaughtered like a Passover lamb on the cross. The reader must not miss the ram, which was offered as a sacrifice in place of Isaac. The Hebrew Bible (Old Testament), especially the books of Genesis, Leviticus, and Numbers, has many references to a ram serving as a burnt offering or sacrifice (Gen 15:9; 29:15–32; Lev 8:18–29; Num 6:14—7:81). While the icon of the sacrificed ram is not employed by Christian Bible (New Testament) authors, it is not difficult to see how appropriate it is, especially as a male fertility image, applied to Christ.

The third reading (Exod 14:15—15:1) is the account of the crossing of the Red Sea by the Israelites after their escape from Egypt. As already mentioned above in the explanation of the Passover, the people are faced with death at the hands of pharaoh and his forces. Through Moses, God divides the sea in two, and the people pass through it to a new life. The Egyptian forces are drowned in their attempt to catch the Israelites, for the sea flows back upon them.

Israel's salvation is seen as a sign of the salvation offered to all people through baptism, the sacramental initiation into the paschal mystery. Both of the prayer options which follow this reading make this clear. In the first prayer, the priest or bishop mentions the waters of rebirth, while the second prayer declares that the crossing through the Red Sea prefigures the font in which people are reborn by water and the Spirit.[5] The prayer ending the

---

3. Ibid., par. 19.
4. Ibid., par. 22.
5. Ibid., par. 26.

series of seven Scripture selections from the Hebrew Bible (Old Testament), makes a direct connection between the references to the paschal mystery in the Hebrew Bible (Old Testament) and in the Christian Bible (New Testament).[6]

BAPTIZED INTO THE PASCHAL MYSTERY

The epistle is taken from Paul's letter to the Romans (6:3–11). It is a reminder that baptism begins tracing the paschal mystery in the life of a Christian. Rhetorically, Paul asks the Romans, "Do you not know that all of us who have been baptized into Christ Jesus were baptized into his death?" (Rom 6:3) Then, he answers by writing, "Therefore we have been buried with him by baptism into death, so that, just as Christ was raised from the dead by the glory of the Father, so we too might walk in newness of life" (Rom 6:4).

In Paul's time, the baptismal pool was often grave-like; it was deep enough for a person to be totally immersed. The candidate, looking like the old Adam, striped off his or her clothes, stepped down into the watery tomb, was buried (metaphorically drowned), was raised up, and walked out of the watery womb to new life, like the second Adam, Christ. Dressed in his or her new white garment, the newly-born Christian began to live a transformed life. Baptism incorporates one into the body of the Christ who suffered, died, and was raised by God. It is called the font of rebirth,[7] and the "Blessing of Baptismal Water" echoes this understanding. The priest or bishop prays that those buried with Christ by baptism into death in the font may rise to life with him.[8] This point is even further emphasized in the instruction given to the congregants before they renew their baptismal promises. The priest or bishop tells them that through the paschal mystery they have been buried with Christ in baptism so that they can walk in newness of life.[9]

The "Blessing of Baptismal Water" prayer illustrates how God uses water as a sign of the grace of baptism which begins paschal mystery spirituality for Christians. The great flood foreshadows regeneration. The crossing of the Red Sea prefigures baptized people. The prayer states that Jesus' baptism in the Jordan River by John was his anointing with the Holy Spirit, and

6. Ibid., par. 30.
7. Ibid., pars. 40, 43.
8. Ibid., par. 46.
9. Ibid., par. 55.

the unique Johannine portrayal of the flowing of blood and water from his side institutes baptism.[10] All of these connections between the Passover in the Hebrew Bible (Old Testament) and the passover in the Christian Bible (New Testament) prepare for this night when throughout the world Christian believers are set apart from worldly vices and led to grace through baptism. Indeed, the sanctifying power of the night dispels wickedness, washes away faults, and restores innocence.[11] It also shouts about paschal mystery spirituality insofar as identifying the role water plays in the unfolding of the paschal mystery in the life of the baptized.[12]

RESURRECTION ACCOUNTS

The gospel for the Easter Vigil is dependent upon the current cycle—A (2020, 2023, 2026, etc.), B (2018, 2021, 2024, etc.), or C (2019, 2022, 2025, etc.). Thus, it consists of the account of the announcement by the angel of the Lord in Matthew's Gospel (28:1–10) in Year A, the empty tomb and the proclamation by the young man in Mark's Gospel (16:1–8) in Year B, or the appearance of two men in Luke's Gospel (24:1–12) who announce the resurrection in Year C.

The author of Matthew's Gospel understands the resurrection to be a theophany, as indicated by the earthquake (Matt 28:2) and the angel's appearance described as being like lightning (Matt 28:3). The angel rolls the stone away from the tomb's entrance to show the two women that Jesus is no longer there. Later, Jesus appears to the two women and sends them on a mission to announce his resurrection to his disciples. In Mark's Gospel, three women find the stone already rolled away from the tomb's entrance. A young man dressed in a white robe declares that Jesus of Nazareth has been raised. However, the women leave and say nothing to anyone! Luke's version features three named women and other unnamed women who find two men in dazzling clothes in Jesus' tomb. The two men remind the women that Jesus had said that he must be handed over, crucified, and rise on the third day. The women leave the tomb and go tell the apostles.

---

10. Ibid., par. 46.
11. Ibid. par. 19.
12. *Rite of Christian Initiation*, par. 210.

The Prayer over the Offerings for the Easter Vigil refers to the paschal mysteries,[13] while the Prayer after Communion refers to the paschal sacrament,[14] and the Solemn Blessing refers to the paschal feast.[15] Thus, there is little room for doubt that the Easter Vigil is focused on the paschal mystery.

REFLECTION

The primary focus of The Easter Vigil in the Holy Night is tracing paschal mystery spirituality in those presented for baptism. When there is no one to be baptized, then, minimally, it is renewing the tracing of paschal mystery spirituality in the lives of the baptized. Seaman tells a story about a family coming to the font during the Easter Vigil. He writes:

> [A] mother and her children had been awaiting baptism for nearly two years. [She] decided she would go first, to show the children . . . how she would enter the waters into which they would follow. After the Blessing of the Water, the bishop helped her into the large, deep baptismal font. He then stepped in himself. All of a sudden, the smallest child ran to the bishop, waving his finger and exclaiming, "Do not drown my mom!" The bishop was quite surprised. He reassured this child that he would not drown the mother. Then, turning to the assembly, the bishop said, "Did everyone hear that? He gets what baptism is about—death, but also, we need to add, new life."[16]

As the bishop clearly states, baptism is immersion into the paschal mystery. The "General Introduction to Christian Initiation" emphasizes that the sacraments of Christian initiation—baptism, confirmation, and Eucharist—join us "to Christ's death, burial, and resurrection. We receive the Spirit . . . and are part of the entire people of God in the celebration of the memorial of the Lord's death and resurrection."[17] More specifically,

> Baptism incorporates us into Christ. . . . [It makes us] a new creation through water and the Holy Spirit. By signing us with the gift

---

13. *Roman Missal*, "Easter Sunday of the Resurrection of the Lord: The Easter Vigil in the Holy Night," par. 61.
14. Ibid., par. 67.
15. Ibid., par. 68.
16. Seaman, "How Does Baptism Change Us?"
17. "General Introduction," par. 1.

of the Spirit, confirmation makes us more completely the image of the Lord and fills us with the Holy Spirit. . . . Finally, coming to the table of the Eucharist, we eat the flesh and drink the blood of the Son of Man so that we may have eternal life. . . . By offering ourselves with Christ, we share in the universal sacrifice, that is, the entire community of the redeemed offered to God by their High Priest, and we pray for a greater outpouring of the Holy Spirit, so that the whole human race may be brought into the unity of God's family.[18]

In other words, during the Easter Vigil, people are initiated into the paschal mystery and paschal mystery spirituality through baptism, confirmation, and Eucharist. What happened to Jesus—suffering, death, resurrection, ascension, and gift of the Spirit—happens for the first time in those being baptized and is renewed in those already baptized. Indeed, the already-baptized have a major role to play in preparing those who seek the sacraments of initiation, referred to as catechumens. According to the *Rite of Christian Initiation of Adults*, they join the catechumens "in reflecting on the value of the paschal mystery."[19] According to the *Rite*, initiation must bear "a markedly paschal character, since the initiation of Christians is the first sacramental sharing in Christ's dying and rising. . . . "[20]

Those preparing for the sacraments of initiation set out on a paschal mystery spirituality journey that can last anywhere from one year to three or more years. According to the *Rite*, they already begin to share through faith in the paschal mystery. This transformation also comes with a change in outlook and behavior; this is the ascension aspect of the paschal mystery.[21] A new perspective is occurring in those seeking baptism as they look forward to celebrating at Easter the paschal mystery of the Lord's suffering, death, and resurrection.[22]

Paschal mystery spirituality reaches its crescendo when those who have prepared for baptism share in Jesus' death and resurrection through immersion in the font.[23] They die with Jesus in the watery tomb, and they rise like Christ from the grave to new life. Then to demonstrate the unity of

---

18. Ibid., par. 2.
19. *Rite of Christian Initiation*, par. 4.
20. Ibid., par. 8
21. Ibid., par. 75:2.
22. Ibid., pars. 114, 134.
23. Ibid., par. 213.

the paschal mystery—suffering, death, resurrection, ascension, and gift of the Spirit—they are immediately confirmed. In other words, the Holy Spirit is poured out on them through water and the anointing with Chrism Oil.[24] Then, they celebrate the memorial of the paschal mystery in the Eucharist for the first time.[25] By eating the body and drinking the blood of Christ they are united to his paschal mystery, even as they are living their own. It cannot be any clearer from a paschal mystery spirituality point of view: What happened to Jesus is happening to those who follow him. The celebration of the sacraments of initiation during the Easter Vigil begins paschal mystery spirituality in the newly initiated and reminds the already initiated how they should be living through suffering, death, resurrection, ascension, and the gift of the Spirit.

1. Like Isaac, how have you passed through death to life?
2. What experience of your life reminds you that you have been baptized into Christ's death? What experience of your life reminds you that you have been raised to newness of life?
3. How do your experiences of resurrection mirror the variety of narratives about it in the Christian Bible (New Testament)?
4. What role—either actively or passively—do you have in living the paschal mystery and demonstrating its spirituality to others?
5. How does the renewal of your baptismal promises during the Easter Vigil fit into your paschal mystery spirituality?

---

24. Ibid., par. 215.
25. Ibid., par. 217.

12

Easter Sunday of the Resurrection of the Lord

EASTER SUNDAY BEGINS THE fifty-day celebration of the resurrection of Jesus. Its primary focus is on the resurrection aspect of the paschal mystery, as can best be seen in the Collect for the Mass during the Day. The priest or bishop says that on this day all remember how Jesus conquered death through his resurrection.[1]

The Scripture selections also focus on the resurrection, but are careful also to mention the suffering and death aspects of the paschal mystery. The first reading, from the Acts of the Apostles (10:34a, 37–43), is part of Peter's speech which inaugurates the Gentile mission before the centurion Cornelius is baptized. Peter recounts the paschal mystery by stating that Jesus was put to death by being hung on a tree, but God raised him on the third day (Acts 10:39–40).

There are two choices for the second reading. The first choice is from the letter to the Colossians (3:1–4). The author exhorts his readers, who have died (Col 3:3) and been raised with Christ (Col 3:1) and whose lives are hidden with Christ in God (Col 3:3), to seek what is above, where Christ is seated at the right hand of God (Col 3:1). They are to think of what is above, not of what is on earth (Col 3:2). What this means is that their

---

1. *Roman Missal*, "Easter Sunday of the Resurrection of the Lord: At the Mass during the Day," par. 72.

Christian lifestyle indicates that they are followers of Jesus, who has been raised and exalted by God.

The second choice for the second reading is taken from the First Letter of Paul to the Corinthians (5:6–8). Paul declares that the paschal lamb, Christ, has been sacrificed (1 Cor 5:7). Now, Christians live a new life. Paul compares this new life to the festival of Unleavened Bread, which followed Passover. Bread was unleavened because yeast was considered to be corruptive.

With this understanding, Paul writes that a little yeast leavens all the dough (1 Cor 5:6). Therefore, those who have been baptized into the paschal mystery of Christ should clear out the old yeast, so that they may become a fresh batch of dough (1 Cor 5:7). Easter is a feast which is to be celebrated not with the old yeast, the yeast of malice and wickedness, but with the unleavened bread of sincerity and truth (1 Cor 5:8). The resurrection leavens all who participate in paschal mystery spirituality.

Following the second reading, the Sequence, a unique hymn probably originating in the Middle Ages, is sung. In the song, references are made to the Paschal Victim, obviously Christ, and to the Lamb who redeems the sheep, another reference to Christ and Christians. Also, death and resurrection are described as fighting a stupendous battle—dualism at its best. But the prince of life, who died, now reigns immoral. The song ends with the proclamation of the paschal mystery, that is, Christ has risen from the dead.[2]

The gospel for Easter Sunday is the account of the empty tomb from John's Gospel (20:1–9). This story begins with a narrative about Mary Magdalene going to the tomb alone and seeing that the stone has been removed from the entrance. She runs to Peter and the other disciple whom Jesus loved (John 20:2) and announces, "They have taken the Lord out of the tomb, and we do not know where they have laid him" (John 20:2). Peter and the other disciple race to the tomb. Peter enters first and observes the burial cloths. The other disciple enters, sees, and believes. Then, the narrator states, " . . . [T]hey did not understand the scripture, that he must rise from the dead" (John 20:9). Since seeing and believing are synonymous throughout the Fourth Gospel, the author places an emphasis on not having to see the empty tomb or the risen Jesus in order to believe (John 20:29).

Instead of this gospel, the priest or bishop may choose to proclaim the gospel from the Easter Vigil, or, if presiding at an Easter afternoon Mass,

---

2. *Lectionary*, Volume I, 357.

the gospel selection from Luke (24:13–35) about Jesus' post-resurrection appearance to the two disciples on the road to Emmaus.

On Easter Sunday the paschal mystery is emphasized through the renewal of baptismal promises, as is done at the Easter Vigil. The congregation is reminded that it is through the paschal mystery that they have been buried with Christ in baptism, so that they may rise with him to a new life.[3]

Preface I of Easter, subtitled *The Paschal Mystery*, proclaims that Christ, the passover, has been sacrificed. He is declared to be the true Lamb who by dying destroyed death and by rising restored life.[4] In the Prayer over the Offerings, the priest or bishop exults with paschal gladness,[5] and declares that the congregants have been renewed by the paschal mysteries.[6]

REFLECTION

Since the primary aspect of the paschal mystery celebrated on Easter Sunday is resurrection, it behooves us to reflect upon the meaning of that word. Most people think of resuscitation when they hear the word *resurrection*. However, resurrection is not resuscitation, which means to revive from unconsciousness or apparent death. In other words, resuscitation refers to what looks like death, but is not really death. Resurrection is on the other side of death. Jesus really died, and God raised him from the dead. In the Symbol, Profession of Faith, or Creed, Christians proclaim that Jesus was crucified, that "he suffered death and was buried, and rose again on the third day."[7] Likewise, in the Apostles' Creed, they profess that he suffered, "was crucified, died, and was buried; . . . on the third day he rose again from the dead."[8]

Before creeds were created, there was Paul. The best presentation of his understanding of resurrection is found in his First Letter to the Corinthians. In chapter 15 he explains to the Corinthians that he is handing on

---

3. *Roman Missal*, "Easter Sunday of the Resurrection of the Lord: The Easter Vigil in the Holy Night," par. 55.

4. Ibid., "Order of Mass," par. 45.

5. Ibid., "Easter Sunday of the Resurrection of the Lord: At the Mass during the Day," par. 73.

6. Ibid., par. 76.

7. Ibid., "Order of Mass," par. 18.

8. Ibid., par. 19.

the good news that Christ died, that he was buried, and that he was raised on the third day (1 Cor 15:3–4). Obviously, there are some in Corinth who doubt the resurrection (1 Cor 15:12–19); Paul presumes resurrection, presenting it as a fact (1 Cor 15:20). In his Letter to the Romans he declares that Jesus "was declared to be Son of God with power according to the spirit of holiness by resurrection from the dead" (Rom 1:4). However, it is not until the end of chapter 15 in First Corinthians that the apostle begins to explain what it is. The metaphor he chooses to use is that of a seed. "What you sow does not come to life unless it dies," he states (1 Cor 15:36). A seed planted in the earth has one type of body, but once it dies and begins to grow it possesses another type of body. "So it is with the resurrection of the dead. What is sown is perishable, what is raised is imperishable" (1 Cor 15:42). He writes, "It is sown a physical body; it is raised a spiritual body. If there is a physical body, there is also a spiritual body" (1 Cor 15:44).

It is important to note that the earliest attempt to describe resurrection acknowledges that it cannot be described! Paul's use of the seed metaphor merely states what it may be like, but it does not tell us what it is. Paul's argument that if there is a physical body, there must be a spiritual body does not tell us what resurrection is; it merely adds another layer to the metaphor. Nevertheless, it does not decrease the apostle's desire "to know Christ and the power of his resurrection and the sharing of his sufferings by becoming like him in his death" (Phil 3:10). Thus, Paul does not know what resurrection is because it is on the other side of death, and he has not been to that realm; he believes that it is some form of transformation through death to new life.

After Paul came the gospel writers. Like Paul, the author of Mark's Gospel has no clue as to what resurrection is; this is demonstrated by the fact that the Markan Jesus makes no post-resurrection appearances in the original ending (Mark 16:8). But also like Paul, the author of this gospel considers it to be some type of transformation or transfiguration (Mark 9:2–3); however, even here the author employs elements of Hebrew Bible (Old Testament) theophanies—particularly the cloud and God's voice—to make his point.[9] The author of Matthew's Gospel understands resurrection to be a theophanic experience as demonstrated with the earthquake (Matt 28:2).[10] He thinks that resurrection is bodily, as when Jesus appears to the women leaving his tomb they take hold of his feet and worship him (Matt

9. Boyer, *Divine Presence*, 26–29, 34–41, 89–95, 113–120.
10. Ibid., 74–6.

28:9). Likewise, the author states that the eleven disciples can see Jesus when he makes his second and last Matthean appearance (Matt 28:17).

The author of Luke's Gospel thinks that resurrection is a bodiless body! The women who go to Jesus' tomb do not find a body (Luke 24:3, 23). Likewise, Peter who goes to the tomb sees the linen cloths in the tomb, but there is no body there (Luke 24:12, 24, 34). The two disciples on the road to Emmaus do not recognize Jesus when he joins them (Luke 24:15–16), but they can see him and hear him (Luke 24:17a, 19a, 25–26), and he joins them for dinner (Luke 24:29) before vanishing from their sight (Luke 24:31). Likewise, after the two disciples return to Jerusalem and report what they experienced (Luke 24:35), Jesus stands among them and speaks to them (Luke 24:36–38, 44–49). In order to prove to them that it is he, he invites them to touch his flesh and bones (Luke 24:39–40) and he eats a piece of broiled fish (Luke 24:42–43). Then, he leads them to Bethany and disappears by ascending into heaven (Luke 24:50–51). Thus, the bodiless body completes his mission on earth. If he had a physical body, to where did he go?

The author of Luke's Gospel also wrote the Acts of the Apostles. In the opening verses of this book, the narrator rehearses the end of the gospel (Acts 1:1–5) and presents Jesus' ascension as a theophany, using the element of a cloud which takes him out of their sight (Acts 1:9).[11] Thus, as in the gospel, the bodiless body completes his mission after spending forty days[12] (Acts 1:3) teaching the disciples in contrast to his ascension on Easter Sunday evening in the gospel.

The author of John's Gospel also considers resurrection to be a bodiless body. In his account of the resurrection, Peter and the beloved disciple go to the tomb at the bidding of Mary Magdalene and see the linen wrappings (John 20:5–7) but no body. Like the two disciples on the road to Emmaus in Luke's Gospel, Mary Magdalene at first does not recognize Jesus when he appears to her (John 20:11–15) until he pronounces her name (John 20:16). Jesus tells her not to hold onto him (John 20:17); the reader presumes that she has embraced him. She makes it clear that he has a body when she tells his disciples that she has seen him (John 20:18).

However, he is also bodiless because he can pass through locked doors (John 20:19), but he also has a body because he speaks to his disciples (John 20:19) and shows them his body (John 20:20) and breathes on them (John

11. Ibid., 34–41.
12. Ibid., 17–18.

20:22). A week later he shows his body to Thomas (John 20:27). In the epilogue, chapter 21, a section added onto John's Gospel by a writer other than the author of most of the previous chapters, Jesus appears to the disciples by the Sea of Tiberias (John 21:1–12a) in a body that they can recognize (John 21:12b–14) and dialogues with Peter (John 21:15–19). Thus, the author of the Fourth Gospel thinks that resurrection is best described as a bodiless body.

The *Catechism of the Catholic Church* is of no real help in this regard. From paragraph 631 to 667, it merely repeats the biblical material examined above and elsewhere in this book about the paschal mystery. It does declare that "the risen body in which [Christ] appears . . . is the same body that had been tortured and crucified, for it still bears the traces of his passion."[13] At the same time, his resurrection "was not a return to earthly life;"[14] "no one was an eyewitness . . . and no evangelist describes it;"[15] "it remains at the very heart of the mystery of faith as something that transcends and surpasses history."[16] Emphasizing its theophanic nature, the *Catechism* states, "Christ's resurrection is an object of faith in that it is a transcendent intervention of God himself in creation and history."[17] Thus, the *Catechism* itself cannot explain what resurrection is because it is on the other side of death.

From physics we learn that there is space in everything. However, the space that exists in everything may not be space at all; it may be God's Spirit, God's free energy that sustains all life and changes all death to life. Daily experiences of letting go, of turning loose of control, are degrees of death before final death. Indeed, we are dying throughout our lives. However, we notice that all those preliminary deaths to final death are spaces filled with grace, energy, or Spirit, and we keep finding new life when we cross through all types of dying to the other side. Jesus was raised by God; he was brought through death to resurrection by uncreated and unearned grace, energy, or Spirit. The Collect for Friday of the Third Week of Easter captures this when the priest or bishop reminds God that those who have come to know the grace of the Lord's resurrection desire, through the Spirit's love, to rise

---

13. *Catechism*, par. 645.
14. Ibid., par. 646.
15. Ibid., par. 647.
16. Ibid.
17. Ibid., par. 648.

to newness of life.[18] If we stand back and observe our experiences, we may begin to notice that the pattern etched into our lives is nothing other than the paschal mystery of Jesus. And by embracing it wholeheartedly, we live paschal mystery spirituality.

1. How do you keep Easter for fifty days?
2. How does celebrating the resurrection leaven (corrupt) you with new life?
3. How is your resurrected life hidden? How is it unleavened?
4. Do the gospel empty tomb stories prove the resurrection for you? How? Why not?
5. What metaphor best captures the meaning of resurrection for you? Explain.
6. How does resurrection fit into your paschal mystery spirituality? How have you experienced resurrection?

---

18. *Roman Missal*, 409.

13

The Ascension of the Lord

THE ASCENSION OF THE Lord is celebrated on the fortieth day of the Easter Season, although in many countries this solemnity is moved to the Seventh Sunday of Easter. Ascension is the fourth aspect of the paschal mystery. Only the author of Luke's Gospel records an ascension of Jesus; the account in Mark (16:15–20) read in Year B forms part of "The Longer Ending" of his gospel, which was not written by the original author but added at a later date. The Matthean selection read in Year A (Matt 28:16–20) is not about an ascension at all, but records Jesus' promise to be with his disciples until the end of the age (Matt 28:20) as he sends them forth to make disciples by baptizing them and teaching them to observe all he has commanded (Matt 28:19–20).

Luke, however, records the ascension of Jesus two times, once in his gospel (Luke 24:46–53), which is read in Year C, and once in his companion volume of the Acts of the Apostles (1:1–11), which is the first reading in all three cycles. However, the accounts do not agree with each other, since the author is not recording history but is interested in making a theological statement. The account found in the gospel portrays the ascension as taking place on Easter Sunday evening. After commissioning the disciples to be witnesses through their preaching, Jesus is taken up to heaven (Luke 24:51). In the gospel, then, the ascension serves to remove from the scene the Jesus who keeps making post-resurrection appearances so that the mission of the disciples can begin. There is no reason to begin a mission of witnessing as long as Jesus is still present in Luke's theological understanding.

In the Acts of the Apostles, the same author portrays the ascension as taking place forty days after Easter. He records that "[a]fter his suffering [Jesus] presented himself alive to [the apostles] by many convincing proofs, appearing to them during forty days and speaking about the kingdom of God" (Acts 1:3). After telling them that they would "receive power when the Holy Spirit" would come upon them, and that they would be his "witness in Jerusalem, in all Judea and Samaria, and to the ends of the earth" (Acts 1:8), Jesus "was lifted up, and a cloud took him out of their sight" (Acts 1:9). Luke's mention of the cloud indicates that he thinks of the ascension as a theophany.[1] The same two men, who had been at the empty tomb (Luke 24:4) re-appear dressed in white garments (Acts 1:10) and state that Jesus will one day come again.

In the Acts of the Apostles, Luke employs the theological concept of the ascension to signal the end of the presence of Jesus on the earth and beginning of time of the church. Employing the Hebrew Bible (Old Testament) sacred time of forty days,[2] he indicates that Jesus continued to give instructions through the Holy Spirit to the apostles whom he had chosen (Acts 1:2). The bond between Jesus and his apostles is sealed during this time, just as the bond between God and his people was sealed during the forty-year sojourn of the Israelites in the desert before entering the promised land and the forty days and nights spent by Moses on God's mountain, where he received the first covenant, which sealed the union between God and his people.

REFLECTION

The focus of Ascension is not on gazing up into the heavens, but on the new vision which we have gained throughout Lent and the first forty days of Easter. The changes we made in our lives during Lent through discipline are lived throughout the Easter Season. By the time of the ascension, a new perspective should be obvious to us. Preface I of the Ascension of the Lord

1. Boyer, *Divine Presence*, 34–41.
2. Ibid., 17–18.

states this best. It says that Christ has ascended, not to distance himself from us, but that we might be confident of following him.[3] In other words, he has given a vision for our lives. By Ascension we should have a different perspective on our lives, our faith, and our world. The changes, which during this sacred time have taken deep root in us, enable us to see as Jesus sees and to continue to live the new life which has been etched in us through our paschal mystery spirituality.

Most people do not like change, and yet we live through liturgical year after liturgical year which is focused on change. In order to get at the transformation that can occur in our lives, sometimes just changing the chair we usually sit on in the living room, den, or dining room gives us a different perspective on the room. Because many church goers sit in the same pew most Sundays, changing both the side of the church and the pew can change our vision of what we do there. Likewise, our Lenten practice might include changing the route we take to work, the grocery store in which we shop, or the gas station at which we stop to fill our car's tank. We can see new things along the way. Such simple transformative experiences have the ability to raise our awareness of other changes that we may need to make in our paschal mystery spirituality. Beware, however, any change will require some suffering, some dying, and some rising before the new vision becomes clear.

The Collect prayed at the Vigil Mass emphasizes the new perspective celebrated in the Ascension of the Lord. The priest or bishop asks God to make us worthy for Christ to live with us now on earth and we with him in heaven.[4] Likewise, the Prayer after Communion asks God to kindle a longing for our heavenly homeland so that we press forward following in Christ's footsteps.[5] At the Mass during the Day, two optional collects are presented. One declares that the Ascension of Christ is our exaltation. It employs the second-generation Pauline concept of Christ as head of the church and people as his body. It asks God to help all follow the head in hope of glory.[6] The second optional Collect asks that we may in spirit dwell already in heavenly realms.[7] In other words, we pray that the ascension aspect of the paschal mystery—the new vision—may already be

3. *Roman Missal*, "Order of Mass," par. 50.
4. Ibid., 431.
5. Ibid.
6. Ibid., 432.
7. Ibid.

ours. As in the Vigil Mass Prayer after Communion, the Mass during the Day Prayer after Communion asks God to grant us Christian hope that will draw us onward to where our nature is united with Christ's.[8] This last idea is echoed in Preface II of the Ascension of the Lord in which the priest of bishop states that Christ's ascension makes us sharers in his divinity.[9]

Thus, on the Ascension during the Easter Season we are reminded of the new vision which we have gained throughout Lent, the Sacred Paschal Triduum, and Easter. Now, we have a different perspective on our lives, and that perspective affects others. The transfiguration that has occurred in us has taken root. Now, we recognize that the paschal mystery of Jesus is the same paschal mystery spirituality that we live every day.

1. What change occurred in your vision or perspective as a result of your latest observance of Lent and Easter?
2. How can you practice changing your vision or perspective on a regular basis?
3. Why is it necessary for the author of Luke's Gospel to include in his account the ascension of Jesus? Why is it important for you to include changing your perspective in your life?
4. In what specific ways does your new vision or perspective affect others?
5. How does ascension fit into your paschal mystery spirituality? How have you experienced ascension?

---

8. Ibid., 433.
9. Ibid., "Order of Mass," par. 51.

14

Pentecost Sunday

VIGIL MASS

ON PENTECOST SUNDAY, THE fiftieth day of the Easter Season, the Easter Season comes to a close. Every aspect of life is guided by the Holy Spirit, Jesus' gift to people. There is a Vigil Mass which can be celebrated in an extended form or a simple form. The extended form is patterned after the Liturgy of the Word of the Easter Vigil. The priest or bishop acknowledges that the congregants are imitating the example of those who persevered in prayer awaiting the Spirit promised by Christ.[1] Six Scripture texts are presented. The first narrates the building of the tower of Babel (Gen 11:1–9). The second is a part of the much longer narrative of Moses on Mount Sinai (Horeb) with the theophanic elements of thunder, lightning, cloud, trumpet blast, smoke, fire, and earthquake (Exod 19:3–8a, 16–20b).[2] The prophet Ezekiel's vision of dry bones coming to life is the third reading (Ezek 37:1–14); after calling upon the four winds to come and breathe life into the dry bones on a plain, the prophet watches as spirit enters into

---

1. *Roman Missal*, "Pentecost Sunday: At the Vigil Mass," par. 3.
2. Boyer, *Divine Presence*, 34–41, 49–73.

them and they come alive. The fourth Scripture text is from the prophet Joel (3:1–5) in which God promises to pour his spirit upon all. The sung response petitions the LORD to send forth his spirit and renew the earth (Ps 104:30).

The Epistle is taken from the Letter of Paul to the Romans (8:22–27). Paul explains how the whole of creation groans, but people have the Spirit who helps them pray and intercedes "with signs too deep for words" (Rom 8:26) with God, who knows the human heart and will through the Spirit. The Alleluia, sung to greet the gospel, becomes a prayer for the Holy Spirit to come and fill the hearts of the faithful and kindle in them the fire of love.

The gospel passage is from John (7:37–39). The writer editorializes, explaining that Jesus' previous statement about those who are thirsty coming to him was about the Spirit, "which believers in him were to receive; for as yet there was no Spirit, because Jesus was not yet glorified" (John 7:39).

In the prayers said in between the first five readings, the priest or bishop prays that God's people, formed by the unity of the Father, the Son, and the Holy Spirit, will be re-created as one.[3] Another prayer identifies the fire and lightning on Mount Sinai (Horeb) with the Spirit and asks that people be aflame with the Spirit poured out on the apostles.[4] After the third reading there are three choices of prayers; one asks that God pour the Holy Spirit on those brought to rebirth by the word of life.[5] The fourth prayer asks that the Holy Spirit make congregants witnesses before the world.[6] The first of two optional Collects explains that the paschal mystery has been celebrated for fifty days, and the other asks that the bright rays of the Holy Spirit may enlighten those born again by God's grace.[7] The Preface explains that Pentecost brings the paschal mystery to completion with the bestowal of the Holy Spirit on all God's adopted children. It also brings to birth the church.[8] The Prayer over the Offerings seeks the blessing of the Spirit, and the Prayer after Communion asks that those who consume the body and blood of Christ will be aflame with the Spirit.[9]

---

3. *Roman Missal*, "Pentecost Sunday: At the Vigil Mass," par. 5.
4. Ibid., par. 6.
5. Ibid., par. 7.
6. Ibid., par. 8.
7. Ibid., 451.
8. Ibid., 456.
9. Ibid., 452.

The simple form of the Vigil Mass reduces the number of biblical texts to three. A choice is made from the first four listed above to serve as the first reading with verses from Psalm 104 (1–2, 24, 35, 27–28, 29, 30) used as a response with the refrain asking God to send out the Spirit and to renew the face of the earth. The second reading is from Paul's Letter to the Romans (8:22–27), and the gospel passage is from John (7:37–39).

MASS DURING THE DAY

The Mass during the Day begins with the Entrance Antiphon taken from the Old Testament (Apocrypha) Book of Wisdom: " . . . [T]he spirit of the Lord has filled the world, and that which holds all things together knows what is said" (Wis 1:7). An alternate antiphon is presented from Paul's Letter to the Romans: " . . . God's love has been poured into our hearts through the Holy Spirit that has been given to us" (Rom 5:5). The Collect asks God to pour the gifts of the Holy Spirit across the earth.[10]

It is no accident that the gospel selection for the Second Sunday of Easter (John 20:19–31), which is the same for all three Sunday cycles, may be proclaimed in a shorter form on Pentecost Sunday (John 20:19–23) in all three cycles. The focus of this unique Johannine section is the gift of the Spirit from Jesus on Easter Sunday evening. The Johannine version of Pentecost occurs on Easter Sunday evening in contrast to the Acts of the Apostles version of Pentecost which occurs fifty days later. According to John, the risen Lord appears to his disciples, who are huddled together behind locked doors, and he breathes on them, saying, "Receive the holy Spirit" (John 20:22). Just as "the LORD God formed man from the dust of the ground and breathed into his nostrils the breath of life; and the man became a living being" (Gen 2:7), so does Jesus breathe the new life of the resurrection into his followers. Just as the prophet Ezekiel stood on the plain filled with dry bones and prophesied to the spirit, saying, "Come from the four winds, O breath, and breathe upon these slain, that they may live. . . . [A]nd the breath came into them" (Ezek 37:9–10), so does Jesus breathe the new life of the resurrection—Spirit—into his followers, and they are set on fire with faith.

The first reading on Pentecost for all three cycles is taken from Luke's Acts of the Apostles. He uses the images of wind, fire, and speaking in

---

10. Ibid., 453.

tongues to write about the effects of the gift of the Holy Spirit. These elements of wind, fire, and tongues form a theophany.[11]

The "sound like the rush of a violent wind" (Acts 2:2) is meant to recall the "wind from God" sweeping "over the face of the waters" in Genesis (1:2) along with the vigil reading from the prophet Ezekiel (37:1–14). Just as God created an orderly universe out of chaos, so does the Spirit of God create an orderly mission through Jesus' disciples. Just as God brought the dry bones to life, so does the Spirit bring Jesus' disciples to life.

The "divided tongues, as of fire" (Acts 2:3), are meant to evoke the presence of God in fire on Mount Sinai (Horeb) (Exod 19:18) as Moses prepared to receive the Law, an echo of another vigil reading (Exod 19:3–8a, 16–20b). Now, God acts in a new covenant, preparing the followers of his Son to go forth and preach the good news of salvation.

Finally, the gift of understanding the various languages is Luke's way of saying that the Lord, who "confused the language of all the earth" while people attempted to build the Tower of Babel (Gen 11:9)—an echo of the vigil's first reading (Gen 11:1–9)—now makes it possible for people to understand the mighty works of God through the Holy Spirit. Even though the apostles' audience are from every place on the face of earth, each hears the apostles speaking in his or her own languages about God's deeds of power (Acts 2:11).

The second reading on Pentecost Sunday, Cycle A, a selection from Paul's First Letter to the Corinthians (12:3–7, 12–13), emphasizes the unified diversity among the members of the body of Christ. "To each [individual] is given the manifestation of the Spirit for the common good" (1 Cor 12:7), writes Paul. He continues, " . . . [A]s the body is one and has many members, and all the members of the body, through many, are one body, so it is with Christ" (1 Cor 12:12). Paul reminds the Corinthians that they were initiated into the body of Christ through baptism, which began the paschal mystery in their lives. " . . . [I]n the one Spirit we were all baptized into one body, . . . and we were made to drink of one Spirit" (1 Cor 12:13). This short selection from First Corinthians on Pentecost Sunday serves to remind all that the Easter Season ends exactly where it began—with the paschal mystery.

In Year B there are two options for the second reading. The first, from Paul's First Letter to the Corinthians (12:3b–7, 12–13) is the same as in Year A. The second option is from Paul's Letter to the Galatians (5:16–25). Paul

---

11. Boyer, *Divine Presence*, 26–29, 64–73, 107–12.

urges his readers to live by the Spirit (Gal 5:16). He says that the desires of the flesh are opposed to the Spirit (Gal 5:17). Those who are led by the Spirit are not subject to the law (Gal 5:18). "If we live by the Spirit," writes Paul, "let us also be guided by the Spirit" (Gal 5:25).

There is the option of the passage from John's Gospel (20:19–23) explained above, and there is another option from John's Gospel (15:26–27; 16:12–15), a pieced-together passage that may be proclaimed in Year B about the Spirit of truth who will guide Jesus' disciples to all truth.

In Year C, besides the optional second reading from First Corinthians (12:3b–7, 12–13), there is the option of a passage from Paul's Letter to the Romans (8:8–17). Paul's presentation is that the Spirit of God dwells in those who have accepted his offer of grace. "If the Spirit of him who raised Jesus from the dead dwells in you, he who raised Christ from the dead will give life to your mortal bodies also through his Spirit that dwells in you" (Rom 8:11). Paul thinks that all who are led by the Spirit are children of God who call God "Abba! Father!" (Rom 8:15) Paul then presents the paschal mystery, explaining how all are joint heirs with Christ if, in fact, they suffer with him so that they may also be glorified with him (Rom 8:17).

The second optional gospel for Year C is from John's Gospel (14:15–16, 23b–26). This passage portrays Jesus promising his disciples another Advocate to be with them. "This is the Spirit of truth . . . " (John 14:17a). Jesus explains, " . . . [T]he Advocate, the Holy Spirit, whom the Father will send in my name, will teach you everything, and remind you of all that I have said to you" (John 14:26). In a similar vein, the Prayer over the Offerings asks that the promise of Jesus, the Holy Spirit, reveal to the congregants the hidden mystery of the sacrifice of bread and wine and lead them to all truth.[12] The Prayer after Communion requests that the gift of the Holy Spirit retain all its force in those who have shared the body and blood of Christ.[13]

REFLECTION

In popular iconography, the Spirit is often depicted as a dove. Sometimes the dove is seen painted on the ceiling over the sanctuary of an old church. Sometimes it is found perched on the shoulder of John the Baptist or resting on top of the baptismal font cover. In the Acts of the Apostles, the

12. *Roman Missal*, 453.
13. Ibid., 457.

metaphors employed are wind, fire, and language. What must be kept in mind in this reflection is that any of those metaphors is an attempt to say what the Spirit is like. Thus, in the endeavor to say something about the Spirit, we begin to realize that there is really nothing that we can speak—there is no metaphor that we can use—that will capture what the Spirit is.

In the prayers of the last week of Easter leading to Pentecost Sunday, various attributes or characteristics of the Spirit are presented. The Holy Spirit is promised to Jesus' apostles;[14] the power of the Holy Spirit is requested from God;[15] the Holy Spirit comes near to dwell graciously within people;[16] the Holy Spirit gathers people together;[17] the Holy Spirit imbues people powerfully with spiritual gifts;[18] the Holy Spirit is light;[19] the Holy Spirit comes to cleanse consciences;[20] and, on the day before Pentecost, the Holy Spirit comes near.[21]

We know there is spirit, because we have experienced it at family gatherings; something happens through conversation, food, and games. There is school spirit in which high school students participate in spirit; that school spirit spills over into various team spirit in football, basketball, baseball, volleyball, etc. A church or parish often possesses a spirit easily recognized by the leaders. And, of course, each one of us is endowed with personality, which, basically, manifests our unique, individual spirit.

Out of all those experiences of spirit, we postulate the existence of the Spirit, which is manifest in all those experiences of spirit, which connects all those experiences of spirit, and in which all those other experiences of spirit participate. In other words, the particular experience serves to manifest the universal experience of Spirit. We might use the metaphors electricity, energy, or inclusivity to describe Spirit. The Spirit is like invisible electricity that surges through the wiring of one's home serving as the source for light, heat, and power. The Spirit is like atomic energy that is released through a nuclear reaction or radioactive decay process; the Spirit energizes all with whom the Spirit reacts. The Spirit is like the unity felt

---

14. Ibid., 437.
15. Ibid., 439.
16. Ibid., 440.
17. Ibid., 441.
18. Ibid., 442.
19. Ibid., 443.
20. Ibid., 443
21. Ibid., 444.

around a campfire or a fire pit; it draws people to the flame, warms them, and instills a sense of inclusivity among them.

Another metaphor for the Spirit is attitude. The Spirit is God's attitude toward the world. God has released a new attitude into the world illustrated by love, compassion, and forgiveness. Love, which is strong as death (Song 8:6b), is like the love of Father and Son emptied out as Spirit. Compassion, sympathy for the suffering of others and willingness to help, springs from spirit united to Spirit. And forgiveness, pardoning others, manifests Spirit. God's new attitude—Spirit—changes everything.

In his Letter to the Romans, Paul writes that he is confident that if the Spirit of God who raised Jesus from the dead dwells in people, he who raised Christ from the dead will give life to mortal bodies also through his Spirit dwelling in people (Rom 8:11). In other words, God's Spirit living within us links the experience of the risen Christ with our own hope for resurrected life. The Spirit is like an energy field that gave the dead Jesus new life. Phiri says that the gift of the Spirit is like another divine emptying. "The self-emptying of the Spirit began with the incarnation and continued when the Spirit took up the dead flesh of Jesus and bound it to the word. The *kenosis* of the Spirit is completed . . . because now the Spirit binds believers to the dead and risen Lord."[22] This is why Paul often refers to believers as temples. God's presence is no longer located in a building; Pentecost celebrates God's presence in people being filled with Spirit—breathed on or fired on. The locus for God's theophany is no longer the Jerusalem Temple; now people are the dwelling place for God in the Spirit, who unites people to Christ, who himself is united in love to the Father.

Phiri writes about the Spirit's role in the paschal mystery. "The role of the Holy Spirit, which was crucial in sanctifying Jesus' humanity and uniting it to the Word in the incarnation, becomes crucial as a gift of the paschal mystery that unites believers to the Son and, in him, to the Father. The Son bestows the same Holy Spirit on believers so that through the Son, with him, and in him they may all be completely united to the Father."[23] This means that through the Spirit, we are in God and God is in us! Through the Spirit, we are participating in that which is much bigger than we are. Grace, another way to speak about spirit, is God in us that wants to find itself. In other words, paschal mystery spirituality is Spirit seeking to connect with spirit.

22. Phiri, "Liturgical Participation," 233–4.
23. Ibid., 235, cf. 242.

1. What metaphor for Spirit catches most of your attention? How does that metaphor apply to your life?
2. How does Pentecost complete your paschal mystery?
3. What experience have you had of the Spirit serving as a guide?
4. What experience have you had of the Spirit bringing unity out of diversity?
5. How does Pentecost fit into your paschal mystery spirituality? How have you experienced Pentecost?

15

Anointing the Sick

WHILE BAPTISM PLUNGES PEOPLE into the paschal mystery and confirmation seals them with the gift of the Holy Spirit (the completion of the paschal mystery) and the Eucharist celebrates the paschal mystery of Jesus connected to the paschal mystery of all, the Sacrament of the Anointing of the Sick unites suffering caused by personal sickness with the suffering dimension of the paschal mystery of Jesus. The "General Introduction" to the *Pastoral Care of the Sick: Rites of Anointing and Viaticum* emphasizes that the sick serve as a reminder to others of higher things. They witness that mortal life must be redeemed through the mystery of Christ's death and resurrection.[1]

The action of anointing the sick flows from the Letter of James, who asks: "Are any among you suffering? They should pray. Are any among you sick? They should call for the elders of the church and have them pray over them, anointing them with oil in the name of the Lord. The prayer of faith will save the sick, and the Lord will raise them up" (Jas 5:13ab, 14–15a). It is obvious that through the Anointing of the Sick, the tracing of the paschal mystery in the lives of the suffering is celebrated. Jesus is the model.

---

1. *Pastoral Care of the Sick*, par. 3.

He took on all the wounds of his passion and shared in all human pain.[2] Paschal mystery spirituality helps people grasp more deeply the mystery of suffering and helps them bear pain with greater courage.[3] Through suffering, the ill "fill up what is lacking in Christ's sufferings for the salvation of the world as [they] look forward to creation's being set free in the glory of the children of God."[4]

This understanding of suffering as sharing in the paschal mystery is not to be understood in a masochistic sense, but neither is it to be dismissed as having no meaning. The seriously ill need God's grace in their time of anxiety, lest they be broken in spirit and weakened in their faith.[5] Through this sacrament, the church commends "those who are ill to the suffering and glorified Lord, that he may raise them up and save them.... Moreover, the church exhorts them to associate themselves willingly with the passion and death of Christ and thus contribute to the welfare of the people of God."[6] After being anointed, the sick are able not only to bear suffering bravely, but also to fight against it.[7]

The *Pastoral Care of the Sick* clearly states the church's understanding that a person's suffering is a participation in the paschal mystery, when it declares, "The sick person will be saved by personal faith and the faith of the church, which looks back to the death and resurrection of Christ, the source of the sacrament's power (see Jas 5:15), and looks ahead to the future kingdom that is pledged in the sacraments."[8] This is also echoed in the rite of celebrating the Anointing of the Sick within Mass, thus combining the remembrance of the paschal mystery of Jesus and the general celebration of it in the life of a Christian with the paschal mystery of the individual, who is suffering from a serious illness.

Throughout the prayers for the Anointing within Mass, the Church refers to Jesus as physician and healer[9] and asks that God transform

---

2. Ibid., par. 2.
3. Ibid., par. 1.
4. Ibid., par. 3.
5. Ibid., par. 5.
6. Ibid.
7. Ibid., par. 6.
8. Ibid., par. 7.
9. Ibid., par. 135A.

weakness by the strength of grace[10] for all who share in Jesus' suffering.[11] A large selection of readings, which treat the themes of suffering, healing, and Eucharist are provided. In the section of *The Roman Missal* which provides "Masses and Prayers for Various Needs and Occasions," one of the prayers for the sick refers to the value of human suffering demonstrated by Jesus.[12]

The Blessing of Oil prayer addresses the God of all consolation and asks that he make the oil a remedy for all who are anointed with it. The priest petitions that God heal the sick in body, in soul, and in spirit, and deliver them from every affliction.[13] The church also prays for comfort for the suffering. In the Prayer after Anointing, the priest prays to the Father, asking that when the sick are afraid, he give them courage; when they are afflicted, he give them patience; when they are dejected, he afford them hope; and when they are alone, he assure them of the support of the community.[14]

One of two Prayers over the Offerings mentions how the bread and wine will be transformed into the risen Lord and reiterates the joining of the individual's sufferings to those of Christ.[15] The other prayer declares that the bread and wine will become the health-giving body and blood of Christ that heals illness and restores life.[16]

All of the above-mentioned themes surrounding suffering are brought together in the Preface. Of particular note is the conjunction of the paschal mystery of Jesus and the paschal mystery of the individual Christian as celebrated in the Eucharist. The priest or bishop mentions Christ the healer, and then he proclaims the paschal mystery. He declares that Christ's resurrection conquered suffering and death and bequeathed his promise of a new and glorious world, where no bodily pain will afflict and no anguish of spirit will exist.[17] He continues by acknowledging the gift of the Holy Spirit who comforts, heals, strengthens, and forgives and offers hope and peace.[18] Through the Eucharist, God gives the risen body of Christ, which serves

---

10. Ibid., par. 136B.
11. Ibid., par. 136A.
12. *Roman Missal*, 1314.
13. *Pastoral Care of the Sick*, par. 140A.
14. Ibid., par. 142A.
15. Ibid., par. 144A.
16. Ibid., par. 144B
17. Ibid., par. 145.
18. Ibid.

as a model of what people will become.[19] Thus, the Anointing of the Sick serves as a celebration of the paschal mystery of Jesus and its manifestation in the life of the ill.

REFLECTION

Our first response to suffering is to stop it. Physical suffering sends us to the medicine cabinet for a pain reliever. Medium suffering sends us to urgent care. Severe suffering sends us to the emergency room. Often physical suffering can be alleviated with an over-the-counter drug, a prescription, or outpatient surgery. There are times when physical suffering requires serious surgery and intensive care in order for healing to take place. Once physical suffering is embraced and care sought, new life can begin to stir.

There is also suffering that results from relationships; sometimes the people we love hurt us or disappoint us. Spouses say hurtful words to each other. Children do not live up to their parents' expectations. The hurting is suffering. In order to remove the suffering, we have to relinquish the hurt by offering forgiveness and making peace. When we have died to the hurt, we discover new life for the relationship.

Likewise, aging entails suffering. As a friend used to say, "Aging is not for the faint of heart." Aging is not for the timid; it requires courage. The only way to age gracefully is to submit to it, to die to it. There are things we cannot do anymore. We do have to act our age and stop pretending that we are younger than we really are. When we let go of pretending, we discover new life being the age we are.

Sometimes we just have to stop in the present and look at all the baggage we carry from the past. Experiences can turn into burdens we haul around with us unless we raise our awareness and consciously decide to lay down the loads we haul. A student friend taught me to find the good in each of the bags we carry and then drop each one. Finding the good in each bag means that we are turning the suffering into death and then passing through death to new life. We are often not even aware of the burdens that cause suffering. Paschal mystery spirituality awakens us to our experiences of good suffering, which we have never had the words to express, never been aware of it in our lives before, or both.

While Jesus stands as the greatest figure of suffering for Christians, throughout history there are others who have suffered. The Hebrews

19. Ibid.

suffered in slavery, until God sent Moses to lead them to freedom. The Israelites suffered in exile once the Babylonians destroyed their kingdom, but God sent the Persian King Cyrus, who permitted them to return home. The first Christians suffered as outsiders both to Judaism and the Roman Empire until Constantine made Christianity a legal religion in his world. As demonstrated throughout the Bible, God takes a stand with those who suffer; God suffers with them. The Anointing of the Sick enacts this truth. The community of believers stands in solidarity with the ill, who are participating in paschal mystery spirituality, and it declares that suffering ends in new life either on this side of the grave or on the other side of it. Anointing the Sick reminds both the ill and those who form a community with them that all share in paschal mystery spirituality throughout their lives.

1. What illness recently made you aware of paschal mystery spirituality?
2. With whose suffering do you most identify? Explain.
3. How have you experienced Jesus as a physician and a healer?
4. How has the suffering aspect of the paschal mystery been traced in your life? What value do you see in human suffering?
5. What is the role of the Spirit in your human suffering? How does that role illustrate paschal mystery spirituality to you?

16

Death, Funeral, and Christian Burial

THE "GENERAL INTRODUCTION" TO the 1989 *Order of Christian Funerals* makes it clear that the paschal mystery is the center of the church's life. It states: "The mystery of the Lord's death and resurrection gives power to all of the church's activity."[1] The death of a Christian, then, is a celebration of the tracing of the paschal mystery in his or her life. According to the "Introduction" to the *Ordo Exsequiarum*, issued in 1969 and emended in 1983, the funeral celebrates Christ's paschal mystery. Those who by baptism were made one body with the dead and risen Christ pass with him from death to life.[2] The *Order of Christian Funerals* also emphasizes that the funeral is the Christian celebration of the dead person's passover from death to life in imitation of Jesus' passover from death to life. Jesus has broken the chains of death principally by the paschal mystery of his passion, resurrection from the dead, and glorious ascension.[3] "The church's liturgical and sacramental life and proclamation of the gospel make this mystery present in the life of the faithful. Through the sacraments of baptism, confirmation, and Eucharist, men and women are initiated into this mystery."[4]

---

1. *Order of Christian Funerals*, par. 2.
2. Ibid., "Appendix 1: *Ordo Exsequiarum*, 1969, Introduction," par. 1.
3. *Order of Christian Funerals*, par. 1.
4. Ibid., par. 2.

In order to support this understanding, the *Order of Christian Funerals* refers first to the Johannine idea that from the side of Christ as he slept the sleep of death upon the cross there came forth the sacrament of the whole church,[5] and second to Paul's letter to the Romans (6:3–5), which explains that baptism into Christ Jesus is baptism into his death and resurrection.[6] Both of these concepts are explained above.

Because the Eucharist celebrates Christ's passover from death to life, the faith of the baptized in the paschal mystery is renewed and nourished through Mass.[7] It is only fitting, then, that at the death of a Christian, whose life of faith was begun in the waters of baptism and strengthened at the eucharistic table, the church intercedes on behalf of the deceased because of its confident belief that death is not the end nor does it break the bonds forged in life.[8] Thus, Mass, the memorial of Christ's death and resurrection, is the principal celebration of the Christian funeral.[9]

The *Order of Christian Funerals* also places an emphasis on the Pauline understanding of the unity of the members of the Church as the body of Christ. This unity is begun in baptism, but celebrated often in Eucharist. The document quotes Paul's reference in 1 Corinthians (10:17) to the one bread of which all partake and which signifies the one body, then it states that at the celebration of the Eucharist the Christian community affirms and expresses the union of the church on earth with the church in heaven in the one great communion of saints. Even though the dead are separated from the living, they are still at one with the community of believers on earth and benefit from their prayers and intercession.[10]

Another aspect of this unity also comes from Paul's First Letter to the Corinthians (12:26)—namely, suffering with others. The *Order of Christian Funerals* states that those who are baptized into Christ and nourished at the same table of the Lord are responsible for one another. Thus, when a member of Christ's body dies, the faithful are called to a ministry of consolation to those who have suffered the loss of one whom they love.[11] The document continues its explanation of this unity of all members of the body of

5. Ibid.
6. Ibid.
7. Ibid., par. 4.
8. Ibid.
9. Ibid., par. 5.
10. Ibid., par. 6.
11. Ibid., par. 8.

Christ by referring to the paschal mystery: Christian consolation is rooted in the hope that comes from faith in the saving death and resurrection of the Lord Jesus Christ.[12]

The death of a Christian and the celebration of the tracing of the paschal mystery in his or her life is the occasion for hope for the living. The *Ordo Exsequiarum* states that the funeral rite brings the consolation of hope to the living.[13] The same document also declares, "As they celebrate the funerals of their brothers and sisters, Christians should be intent on affirming their hope for eternal life."[14] The *Order of Christian Funerals* also makes this point.[15]

The dead also hoped for resurrection.[16] The funeral becomes the occasion to proclaim the belief that all the faithful will be raised up and reunited in the new heavens and a new earth, where death will be no more.[17] This hope is expressed first in the "Prayer of Commendation," when the minister commends the deceased to the Father in the sure and certain hope that with all who died in Christ, the deceased will rise.[18] In another optional "Prayer of Commendation," the minister commends the deceased to the Lord; the deceased looks dead but lives forever in the Lord's sight.[19]

In the "Prayer over the Place of Committal," the church particularly expresses her hope in the resurrection of the dead. In one prayer, the minister declares that Jesus' three days in the tomb hallows the graves of all who believe and makes the grave a sign of hope and promise of the resurrection.[20] And in another prayer, the minister declares that all present place their trust and hope in the living God that one day they will live with him in heaven.[21]

The church's hope in the resurrection of the dead is also made clear in the words of committal. In one formula, the minister commits the body of the deceased to the earth trusting that Christ will one day change it to

---

12. Ibid.
13. Ibid., "Appendix 1: *Ordo Exsequiarum*, 1969, Introduction," par. 1.
14. Ibid., par. 2.
15. *Order of Christian Funerals*, par. 7.
16. Ibid., "Appendix 1: *Ordo Exsequiarum*, 1969, Introduction," par. 1.
17. *Order of Christian Funerals*, par. 6.
18. Ibid., par. 175A.
19. Ibid., par. 175B.
20. Ibid., par. 218A.
21. Ibid., par. 218C.

be like his body in glory.[22] And in another formula, the minister begins by proclaiming the sure and certain hope of the resurrection before committing the body of the deceased to the earth from which it is made.[23]

The church's hope in the resurrection as a result of the paschal mystery of Jesus is stated most clearly in the "Concluding Prayer of the Rite of Committal." The minister declares that it was through Jesus' death on the cross that he destroyed death, through his rest in the tomb that he hallowed the graves of believers, and through his resurrection that he restored eternal life.[24]

The various readings, rituals, and prayers of the funeral liturgy closely parallel those of baptism. This should come as no surprise, since the first celebration of the paschal mystery in baptism is rightly paralleled in the final celebration of it in death. The readings from the word of God proclaim the paschal mystery, convey the hope of being gathered together again in God's kingdom, teach remembrance of the dead, and acknowledge paschal mystery spirituality.[25] The readings also tell of God's designs for a world in which suffering and death will relinquish their hold on all whom God has called his own.[26] The psalms, used as responses between Scripture texts, express the suffering and pain, the hope and trust of people of every age and culture. They sing of faith in God, of revelation and redemption.[27]

In order to compliment the proclamation of the Scriptures, a *Book of the Gospels* or a Bible can be placed on the coffin as a sign that Christians live by the word of God and that fidelity to that word leads to eternal life.[28] While this is being done, the minister explains that the deceased cherished the gospel and asks that Christ welcome him or her to eternal life.[29] This rite echoes the *Rite of Christian Initiation of Adults*' "Presentation of a Bible" found in the "Rite of Acceptance into the Order of Catechumens," a step taken by adults to begin their preparation for baptism.[30]

---

22. Ibid., par. 219A.
23. Ibid., par. 219B.
24. Ibid., par. 222B.
25. Ibid., "Appendix 1: *Ordo Exsequiarum*, 1969, Introduction," par. 11.
26. *Order of Christian Funerals*, par. 22.
27. Ibid., par. 25.
28. Ibid., par. 38.
29. Ibid., par. 400:1.
30. *Rite of Christian Initiation*, par. 64.

The homily, which follows the readings, is also to be focused on the paschal mystery of the Lord, as proclaimed in the Scripture texts.[31] The homilist should help the members of the assembly to understand that the mystery of Jesus' victorious death and resurrection were present in the life and death of the deceased and that these mysteries are active in their own lives as well.[32]

On the day of his or her baptism, the deceased was given a candle, which had been lit from the Paschal Candle, with the instruction to walk always as a child of the light and to keep the flame of faith alive in his or her heart.[33] It is fitting, then, that the Paschal Candle is placed beforehand near the position the coffin will occupy since it reminds the faithful of Christ's victory over death and of their share in that victory by virtue of their initiation. Furthermore, the Paschal Candle recalls the Easter Vigil when the candle is lit for the first time as people await the Lord's resurrection.[34]

Through the waters of baptism, the deceased was plunged into the paschal mystery. During the funeral liturgy, blessed water reminds the assembly of the saving waters of baptism and the deceased's baptism.[35] The sprinkling of the coffin is a reminder that through baptism the person was marked for eternal life.[36] The prayer said by the minister when sprinkling the coffin with water also expresses the baptismal theme of dying and rising with Christ in baptism and now sharing eternal glory.[37]

Another connection between baptism and death is made through the use of the pall, a large, white rectangular piece of cloth used to cover the coffin during the funeral Mass. The pall is a reminder of the baptismal garment of the deceased and a sign of the Christian dignity of the person.[38] The pall, signifying life in Christ,[39] and used to clothe the coffin, should call to mind the formulary said by the minister when giving the newly baptized his or her white garment after baptism. The person became a new creation through baptism and clothed himself or herself in Christ. The person was

---

31. *Order of Christian Funerals*, par. 27.
32. Ibid.
33. *Rite of Christian Initiation*, par. 230.
34. *Order of Christian Funerals*, par. 35.
35. Ibid., par. 36
36. Ibid., par. 147.
37. Ibid., par. 160.
38. Ibid., par. 38.
39. Ibid., par. 133.

told to bring that garment into everlasting life[40]—which he or she has now done.

As stated above, before an adult is baptized, he or she enters into a period of preparation which is known as the catechumenate. The "Rite of Acceptance into the Order of Catechumens" includes a ritual of "Signing of the Forehead." The cross is traced on the forehead of the candidates.[41] As this is being done the minister declares that Christ strengthens the catechumen with the sign of his love.[42] Thus, it is fitting that during the funeral liturgy a cross may be placed on the coffin as a reminder that the Christian is marked by the cross in baptism and through Jesus' suffering on the cross is brought to the victory of his resurrection.[43] The words said by the minister, while placing the cross on the coffin, further clarify this understanding that the deceased received the sign of the cross in baptism and now he or she shares in Christ's victory over death.[44] In the case of a child who died before baptism, the minister declares the cross a sign of hope and love.[45]

The various prayers used during the different rituals comprising the *Order of Christian Funerals* proclaim the paschal mystery and echo the suffering themes of the Scriptures. The paschal mystery is made explicit in one prayer for the mourners in which the minister proclaims that by dying Christ destroyed death and by rising restored life.[46] In one of the "Prayers for the Dead" which echoes Paul's First Letter to the Corinthians (15:20), the minister likewise proclaims that Jesus' death on the cross and his resurrection from the dead makes him the first fruits for all the dead.[47]

Through the paschal mystery Jesus saved people. This is expressed through a reference to Jesus as the passover lamb, as explained above, and as the triumphant lamb of the Book of Revelation in a prayer which concludes the General Intercessions. The minister states that the blood of the Lamb, Jesus, purchased the lives of people.[48] The same idea is expressed in

---

40. *Rite of Christian Initiation*, par. 229.
41. Ibid., par. 54.
42. Ibid., par. 55A.
43. *Order of Christian Funerals*, par. 38.
44. Ibid., par. 400:2.
45. Ibid., par. 400:3.
46. Ibid., par. 399:1.
47. Ibid., par. 398:5
48. Ibid., par. 167A.

another prayer, when the minister says that by the death and resurrection of Jesus, people are redeemed.[49]

Jesus participated in the paschal mystery willingly, according to Paul and Hebrews. A "Concluding Prayer" from the *Order of Christian Funerals* also emphasizes this theme. The minister, addressing the Lord Jesus, declares that he willingly gave himself to death so that all might pass from death to life.[50] Preface II for the Dead states the same idea, declaring that Christ accepted death so that all might escape from dying; he chose to die so that all might live forever.[51] What happened to Jesus—suffering, death, and resurrection—is celebrated in the funeral liturgy as having already happened, but not in total fullness, to the deceased. In one Collect the priest declares that those who have faith profess that Christ died and rose again. Then, he prays that the deceased, through the paschal mystery, may rejoice to rise again through Christ.[52] This same idea is also expressed in Preface I for the Dead; in Christ the hope of resurrection dawned so that those saddened by the certainty of dying may be consoled by the promise of immortality to come.[53] Preface III for the Dead declares that Christ is the life of the human race and the resurrection of the dead.[54] And Preface IV for the Dead declares that those redeemed by the death of Christ will be raised to the glory of his resurrection.[55] Finally, Preface V for the Dead declares that God's compassion and grace calls the dead back into life.[56]

This means that lives are framed by the paschal mystery from the day of baptism to the day of death—and even beyond the grave! Preface IV for the Dead explains this as being summoned to birth by God and commanded by him to return to the earth from which one came.[57] In slightly different words, another prayer makes a direct reference to the mystery of the cross and God's promise to share in the mystery of Christ's resurrection.[58]

---

49. Ibid., par. 398:6.
50. Ibid., par. 80A.
51. *Roman Missal*, "Order of Mass," par. 79.
52. Ibid., 1371.
53. Ibid., "Order of Mass," par. 78.
54. Ibid., par. 80.
55. Ibid., par. 81.
56. Ibid., par. 82.
57. Ibid., par. 81.
58. Ibid., 1386.

One particular celebration of the funeral liturgy can consist of the "Office for the Dead," either morning prayer, evening prayer, or both. Members of the Christian community gather to offer praise and thanks to God especially for the gifts of redemption and resurrection, to intercede for the dead, and to find strength in Christ's victory over death.[59] The office for the dead is "a sign of faith and hope in the paschal mystery."[60]

Morning prayer's focus is the resurrection of Jesus. It relates the death of the Christian to Christ's victory over death and affirms the hope that those who have received the light of Christ at baptism will share in that victory.[61] Evening prayer's focus is on the Christian community's recollection of the cross and Christ's saving works of redemption.[62] During evening prayer, the community gives thanks to God for the gift of life received by the deceased.[63]

No matter what rites or prayers are chosen for a funeral liturgy, the *Order of Christian Funerals* conveys the over-arching theme that suffering, death, and resurrection are the ways that the Christian shares in the paschal mystery. This is particularly emphasized in some of the forty-seven "Prayers for the Dead" section of the book. In a prayer for someone who died after a long illness, the minister declares that God called the deceased to serve him in weakness and pain and, in so doing, shared the cross.[64] In a similar prayer for one who died after a long illness, the minister acknowledges the deceased's great suffering, and God is asked to see the deceased's suffering as redemptive.[65] And the same theme is found in a third prayer for one who died after a long illness. After referring to God as the water for thirst and manna in the desert, the minister praises God for bringing the deceased's suffering to an end and asks him to raise him or her to new life.[66] In a prayer for a person who died by suicide, the minister mentions both the cross and the resurrection. He says that God strengthens by the mystery of the cross and resurrection.[67]

59. *Order of Christian Funerals*, par. 349.
60. Ibid., par. 368.
61. Ibid., par. 350.
62. Ibid., par. 351.
63. Ibid.
64. Ibid., par. 398:39.
65. Ibid., par. 398:40.
66. Ibid., par. 398:41.
67. Ibid., par. 398:45.

Christ Our Passover Has Been Sacrificed

The purpose of the *Order of Christian Funerals* is to celebrate the paschal mystery which was begun in the life of the deceased in baptism, which was celebrated repeatedly in Eucharist throughout the deceased's life, and which is brought to completion in death, while waiting in hope for the fullness of the resurrection. Just as in baptism there are multiple signs and symbols which proclaim the paschal mystery, so are there present many liturgical signs and symbols affirming Christian belief and hope in the paschal mystery in the celebration of the funeral rites.[68]

REFLECTION

In the prophet Isaiah, there is recorded "[a] writing of King Hezekiah of Judah [716–687 BCE], after he had been sick and had recovered from his sickness" (Isa 38:9). What concern us here about Hezekiah's writing are the multiple metaphors he uses for death. His sickness brings him to the noontide of his days (Isa 38:10a), indicating that he thinks his life is only at midday or half over. His illness has brought him to the gates of Sheol (38:10b), the bottom level of a three-storied universe and where the dead live. He laments the fact that he will no longer see God on the second level of the three-storied universe—the earth—where mortals live (Isa 38:11).

He compares his life to a shepherd's tent that is taken down (Isa 38:12a) and to the last thread cut by a weaver at the loom (Isa 38:12b). Hezekiah feels that from day to night his life is coming to an end (Isa 38:12c). Next, he compares his imminent death to a lion breaking his bones (Isa 38:13), his clamoring to that of a swallow or a crane, and his moaning to that of a dove (Isa 38:14a). Being located on the second level of the universe, he looks up to the top level, where God lives, but his eyes are weary looking upward (Isa 38:14b), and he feels oppressed by his sickness (Isa 38:14c). He cannot sleep because his illness makes him bitter (Isa 38:15b). His prayer is that God will restore him to health and life (Isa 38:16b).

Returning to the gates of Sheol, he declares that God had held back his life from the pit of destruction (Isa 38:17b), because death cannot praise God and those there do not hope for his faithfulness (Isa 38:18). Only the living thank the LORD for having preserved life, just like Hezekiah is doing at the end of his prayer (Isa 38:19).

While Hezekiah's metaphors for death are cultural and dated, they are rich! When compared to the simple passed or went home or passed away

---

68. Ibid., par. 21.

metaphors used for death in our culture, they approach death's explanation from a variety of points of view. Hezekiah's metaphors enrich our understanding of the paschal mystery. His suffering through illness brought him to the very edge of death, and he passed through death to new life, to new vision, to new hope. For the Christian, Jesus' death on the cross becomes the model of how to die gracefully and faithfully in trust of God. Thus, death is not to be feared. By living paschal mystery spirituality we know that we are dying throughout our lives. If we remain faithful to God, like Jesus, God remains faithful to us, and death is not the end. Our last passing over, for which we will have practiced and prepared throughout our lives, will, hopefully, be our best. Paschal mystery spirituality offers hope in a culture that often considers death the end of everything.

One of our greatest fears is being forgotten after death. We see this often in promises made by the living to never forget someone recently deceased. The simple fact is that all of us will be forgotten ultimately. To prove this all one has to do is walk through an old cemetery. Those buried there two hundred, one hundred, even fifty years ago are long forgotten, except for their names on their headstones if the weather hasn't worn even that away. Even the greatest who have walked the earth are remembered by few, if any. Getting in contact with this understanding can set us free to come to a deeper appreciation not only of death, but of paschal mystery spirituality.

Every time the Symbol, Profession of Faith, or Creed is said believers declare that they do not believe that death is the end. In fact they declare that they look forward to the resurrection of the dead and the life of the world to come.[69] In the Apostles' Creed believers declare their belief in the resurrection of the body and everlasting life.[70] Paschal mystery spirituality, based on our lifetime experiences of death and resurrection, leads us to declare that what happened to Jesus is happening to us. In other words, life is always changing, but it is never ended—even though we may be forgotten.

1. What does a Christian funeral celebrate for a deceased person? What does it celebrate for the living?

2. How is a cemetery a paradoxical place of death and life? How is a grave a sign of hope and a promise of resurrection for you?

3. How are baptism and its signs referenced in a funeral? Why use the same signs for both baptism and death?

69. *Roman Missal*, "Order of Mass," par. 18.
70. Ibid., par. 19.

4. In general, why should a funeral be a happy occasion?

5. Why is Eucharist celebrated as part of a funeral? What is the connection between Eucharist and the deceased? How has a funeral Eucharist helped to foster your paschal mystery spirituality?

6. What is your favorite metaphor for death? What does it disclose about death? What does it hide about death?

7. When and how have you celebrated paschal mystery spirituality during a funeral?

17

Special Celebrations

Although Palm Sunday of the Passion of the Lord, The Sacred Paschal Triduum, and the Easter Season (including Ascension and Pentecost) most intensely focus on the paschal mystery, the rest of the liturgical year is also permeated with it. For Christians, the question is this: How do they, as the body of Christ, live the paschal mystery—that is, remember it, embody it, and celebrate it?

The yearly cycle and rhythm of the liturgical year is designed to put all in contact with the paschal mystery in their daily lives. This is made clear in the "Universal Norms on the Liturgical Year and the Calendar": The paschal mystery is celebrated every Sunday "and once a year in the great Paschal Solemnity, together with [Christ's] blessed passion. In fact, throughout the course of the year the Church unfolds the entire mystery of Christ. . . ."[1]

During the liturgical year, there are some feasts with prayers and Scripture texts which emphasize some or all of the aspects of the paschal mystery more than others. What follows is not meant to be exhaustive, but

---

1. *Roman Missal*, "Universal Norms," par. 1.

a sampling of paschal mystery spirituality which permeates the church calendar.

PRESENTATION OF THE LORD

On February 2, the church celebrates the Feast of the Presentation of the Lord, which marks the fortieth day after Christmas. Before the Eucharist is celebrated, candles are blessed and a type of mini-Easter Vigil is celebrated. While the feast commemorates the fulfillment of the prophet Malachi's prophecy (Mal 3:1–4) through the presentation of Jesus in the temple and his recognition by Simeon and Anna (Luke 2:22–40), the second reading from Hebrews (2:14–18) states, "Because [Jesus] himself was tested by what he suffered, he is able to help those who are being tested" (Heb 2:18). That this feast is a celebration of the paschal mystery is made clear in the Prayer over the Offerings which refers to Christ as the Lamb without blemish.[2]

BODY AND BLOOD OF CHRIST

On the second Sunday following Pentecost, the Solemnity of the Body and Blood of Christ is celebrated. This day echoes Holy Thursday's focus on the Eucharist as the celebration of the paschal mystery. The Collect refers to the Eucharist as a memorial of Jesus' passion.[3] In Cycle A, the gospel selection is from the bread of life discourse in John's Gospel (6:51–58). The emphasis is placed on Jesus being the "living bread that came down from heaven" (John 6:51). The Johannine Jesus declares that "[w]hoever eats of this bread will live forever" (John 6:51) and that he "will raise them up on the last day" (John 6:54). In other words, the person who eats the Eucharistic bread will have the paschal mystery traced in his or her life not only through communion, but also through the Eucharist, which is the memorial of Jesus' paschal mystery. The unity of the body of Christ, which is brought about through the breaking of bread and the sharing of the cup, is emphasized in the second reading from Paul's First Letter to the Corinthians (10:16–17).

In Cycle B, the gospel selection is from Mark's account of Jesus' Passover supper with his disciples (Mark 14:12–16, 22–26), which is also read on Palm Sunday of the Passion of the Lord in Cycle B. The author of this

2. *Roman Missal*, 820.
3. Ibid., 499.

gospel does not develop the concept of the paschal mystery like John's Gospel does, but he does mention that Jesus' final supper took place "[o]n the first day of Unleavened Bread, when the Passover lamb is sacrificed" (Mark 14:12), which would have been a Thursday according to Mark's order of events.

The same selection used for Holy Thursday's second reading from Paul's First Letter to the Corinthians (11:23–26) is used as the second reading for Cycle C. It is complimented by the gospel selection from Luke (9:11–17), the narrative about the feeding of the five thousand. Luke records that Jesus, after " . . . taking the five loaves and the two fish, . . . looked up to heaven, and blessed and broke them, and gave them to the disciples to set before the crowd" (Luke 9:16). These words echo the Lukan Jesus' words of institution of the Eucharist (Luke 22:19)—read on Palm Sunday of the Passion of the Lord, Year C—as well as the post-resurrection words spoken before breaking bread with two disciples in Emmaus (Luke 24:30). These similarities in wording serve one of Luke's themes, namely, that Jesus shares meals with his disciples, tax collectors, prostitutes, and other sinners.

The Preface for this Mass states the mythology that it was at the last supper with his apostles that Jesus established the saving memorial of the cross, that is, the paschal mystery, because he offered himself to the Father as the unblemished lamb.[4] The mythology covers the Synoptic Gospels of Mark, Matthew, and Luke, but does not cover John's Gospel in which Jesus does not eat a Passover supper with his apostles!

SOLEMNITY OF THE SACRED HEART

On the Friday following the Solemnity of the Body and Blood of Christ, or the Friday following the second Sunday after Pentecost, the church celebrates the Solemnity of the Most Sacred Heart of Jesus. In all three cycles, the Scripture texts focus on the love of God and the love of Christ. However, the gospel selection for Cycle B is a section of John's passion account, which is read on Good Friday, namely the narrative of the soldier piercing the side of the dead Jesus and blood and water flowing forth (John 19:31–37). As stated above, this passage has been understood to signify the birth of the sacraments of Eucharist (blood) and baptism (water), both of which are celebrations of the paschal mystery.

---

4. Ibid., 500; "Order of Mass," par. 61.

These ideas are summarized best in the Preface for this Mass. The paschal mystery is presented through the recalling of Jesus' cross, which demonstrated his love, and the blood and water, which flowed from his pierced side, as recorded only in John's Gospel.[5]

ASSUMPTION OF THE BLESSED VIRGIN MARY

On this solemnity, August 14, the church celebrates the paschal mystery of Christ in the suffering, death, resurrection, ascension, and gift of the Spirit traced in his mother. Both a Vigil Mass and Mass during the Day set of prayers are given in *The Roman Missal*. Likewise, the Lectionary presents a different set of Scripture texts for the Vigil and for the Day.

The Vigil Mass celebrates the tracing of the paschal mystery in Mary's life through her exaltation and triumph with Christ. She has been raised to the special grace of glory through the paschal mystery of her Son.[6] The reference here is to the doctrine that "when the course of her earthly life was finished, [Mary] was taken up body and soul into heavenly glory, and exalted by the Lord . . . , so that she might be the more fully conformed to her Son. . . . "[7] The Preface also emphasizes this point, referring to Mary as the beginning of the church and the image of the church coming to perfection through Christ's paschal mystery.[8]

The Scripture texts present Mary as a bearer of divine presence like the ark of the covenant contained the divine presence (1 Chr 15:1—16:3). Furthermore, she is a model of mortality being clothed with immortality and of death being swallowed in victory through the paschal mystery of her Son (1 Cor 15:54b–57).

The Collect for the Mass during the Day mentions that God assumed Mary, body and soul, into heavenly glory.[9] The same mention is made in the Prayer over the Offerings,[10] and the Prayer after Communion that also petitions God to bring all to the glory of the resurrection.[11]

---

5. Ibid., 503–4.
6. Ibid., 927.
7. *Catechism*, par. 966.
8. *Roman Missal*, 930.
9. Ibid., 926.
10. Ibid.
11. Ibid., 930.

The Scripture texts for the Mass equate the woman clothed with the sun, with the moon beneath her feet, and on her head a crown of twelve stars (Rev 11:19a; 12:1–6a, 10a) with Mary's assumption into heaven. However, it is the passage from Paul's First Letter to the Corinthians which proclaims the paschal mystery. The apostle writes that "Christ has been raised from the dead" and "so all will be made alive in Christ, . . . each in his own order" (1 Cor 15:20–23). The interpretation makes clear that Mary follows Christ as the second person to experience the totality of the paschal mystery. In the words of Luke's Gospel, the Almighty has done great things for Mary (Luke 1:49). Thus, Mary is presented as the first person after Christ to have died and been raised by God, that is, to have experienced the totality of the paschal mystery.

EXALTATION OF THE HOLY CROSS

The feast which most echoes the paschal mystery is that of the Exaltation of the Holy Cross on September 14. The prayers and readings assigned to this day are reminders of Palm Sunday of the Passion of the Lord and Friday of the Passion of the Lord. The second reading is the same as that on Palm Sunday—the selection from Paul's letter to the Philippians (2:6–11). This ancient Christian hymn focuses on Jesus, who "humbled himself and became obedient to the point of death—even death on a cross" (Phil 2:8). The same idea is expressed in the Collect, which mentions that God willed that Jesus undergo the cross.[12]

Jesus' exaltation on the cross is the focus of the gospel selection, chosen from Jesus' dialogue with Nicodemus in John's Gospel (3:13–17), and complimented by the source of John's image—Moses' placement of the bronze serpent on a pole—in the book of Numbers (21:4–9). An in-depth explanation of John's view of Jesus' exaltation on the cross can be found above.

The Prayer over the Offerings for the Mass on this day emphasizes the oblation which was once offered on the cross,[13] while the Preface explicitly proclaims the paschal mystery; where death arose from a tree, life springs

---

12. Ibid., 946.
13. Ibid.

forth from the wood of the cross.[14] The Prayer after Communion mentions redemption, resurrection, through the wood of the life-giving cross.[15]

OUR LADY OF SORROWS

The day after the Feast of the Triumph of the Cross the church honors the Blessed Virgin Mary as Our Lady of Sorrows. The emphasis on Mary's sharing in the paschal mystery is presented in the Collect, which mentions Jesus being lifted high on the cross and his mother standing close by and sharing his suffering, that is, participating in his Passion,[16] an event narrated only in John's Gospel (19:25b–27). The Prayer over the Offerings also mentions Mary standing by the cross.[17]

That this memorial has connections with Good Friday is indisputable, since the first reading for this memorial (Heb 5:7–9) is a shortened version of the second reading on Good Friday (Heb 4:14–16, 5:7–9) and one of the two gospel selections for this memorial (John 19:25–27) is a selection from John's passion account (John 18:1—19:42), which is proclaimed on Good Friday.

The first reading emphasizes the obedient suffering of Jesus, when the author records, "Although he was a Son, he learned obedience through what the suffered; and having been made perfect, he became the source of eternal salvation for all who obey him" (Heb 5:8–9). John's Gospel uniquely portrays Jesus' unnamed mother "standing near the cross" (John 19:25b), as already noted above. Jesus entrusts her to the care of the disciple whom Jesus loved, and he entrusts the disciple to her care (John 19:26–27).

CHRIST THE KING

The last Sunday in the Season of Ordinary Time is the Solemnity of Our Lord Jesus Christ, King of the Universe. This celebration usually falls on the second-to-last or last Sunday of November. While the emphasis of the celebration is on the kingship of Christ, the readings and prayers for this day cannot help but mention the paschal mystery.

14. Ibid., 947–8.
15. Ibid., 948.
16. Ibid., 949.
17. Ibid.

In Cycle A, the second reading focuses on how people come to share in the paschal mystery through Jesus. Paul writes to the Corinthians: " . . . Christ has been raised from the dead, the first fruits of those who have died. For since death came through a human being, the resurrection of the dead has also come through a human being; for as all die in Adam, so all will be made alive in Christ" (1 Cor 15:20–22).

In Cycle B, the second reading refers to " . . . Jesus Christ, the faithful witness, the firstborn of the dead . . . [who] freed us from our sins by his blood . . . " (Rev 1:5). The Prayer over the Offerings echoes this idea of the paschal mystery reconciling the human race to God.[18] The gospel is a selection from John's passion account, which is read on Good Friday. It consists of some of the dialogue between Jesus and Pilate about kingship and truth (John 18:33–37).

In Cycle C, the second reading is chosen from the letter to the Colossians. The author quotes an ancient Christian hymn, which states that through Jesus, God reconciled all things, "making peace through the blood of his cross" (Col 1:20). The reference to the reconciliation which was accomplished by the paschal mystery is echoed in the Preface for this day. It refers to the paschal mystery when it states that Jesus offered himself on the altar of the cross as a spotless sacrifice to bring peace and accomplish reconciliation.[19] The gospel selection for this cycle is taken from Luke's passion account, which is read in its entirety in Cycle C on Palm Sunday. The selection consists of the uniquely Lukan dialogue between Jesus and the thieves who were crucified with Jesus (Luke 23:35–43).

MARTYRS

Besides the selection of special celebrations indicated above, the church remembers various saints throughout the liturgical year. Out of these countless men and women, who are held up as models of universal holiness, are the martyrs. Their day of martyrdom is referred to as their birthday, the day they were born into eternal life. *The Constitution on the Sacred Liturgy* of Vatican Council II states the reason for the church's esteem for the martyrs: "By celebrating their anniversaries the Church proclaims achievement of

---

18. Ibid., 505.
19. Ibid., 506–8.

the paschal mystery in the saints who have suffered and have been glorified with Christ."[20]

REFLECTION

Most people mark some special celebrations in their lives that are permeated with paschal mystery spirituality. For example, all of us have an annual birthday. The day we were born is also the day we died. In fact, as our parents made love to each other and died to each other, we were conceived. Then when nine months had passed, we left the womb, dying to its environment, and coming to life in a world we had not known before. Thus, even before baptism we are engaged in the eternal and universal process of suffering, death, and new life.

When be begin paying attention to this deep truth, we notice that anniversaries mark occasions for dying and new life. Marriage anniversaries celebrate the dying to self and rising to new life in which a couple has been engaged since the day each person promised the other to celebrate paschal mystery spirituality. An anniversary marking a job is the day a person died to one place of work and rose to a new life in another. When deacons, priests, and bishops celebrate the anniversary of their ordination, they remember the day they lay prostrate on the floor to indicate that they were dying to their previous way of life and then rose to a new way of life in ordained ministry.

On Mother's Day and Father's Day every year we honor our parents both living and dead. Parenting is full of dying and new life. Parents die to what they would like to do in order to keep children fed, clothed, housed, and alive. Parents sacrifice buying a new appliance in order to send their children on a trip or to a summer camp. They die to getting a good night's sleep in order to preserve the lives of their sick children by taking care of them. Parents who practice dying and new life regularly are living paschal mystery spirituality.

Paschal mystery spirituality not only fosters a rhythm for our lives, but it also offers us the opportunity to enter into wholeness, the "seamless integration of body, mind, heart, and spirit."[21] According to Buber, "wholeness is a direction of movement that comes and goes in particular

---

20. "Constitution," par. 104.
21. Kramer, *Martin Buber's Spirituality*, 48.

concrete moments,"[22] and that is exactly what paschal mystery spirituality is designed to do. Uniting the paschal mystery of Jesus to our own paschal mystery plunges us into the deeper truth that "wholeness involves both surrender and action, grace and will, mutuality [between the person and God] . . . , and embodies the presence of freedom."[23] We become whole (and holy) "by truly entering into engagement with the world, with others, [and] with God"[24] through suffering, death, resurrection, ascension, and the gift of the Spirit. That's paschal mystery spirituality, and it is God-infused throughout our lives if we but take the time to awaken to its truth.

1. How do you, as a member of the body of Christ, live the paschal mystery—that is, remember it, embody it, and celebrate it?
2. How does your birthday and anniversaries celebrate paschal mystery spirituality?
3. Which special liturgical year celebration best illustrates the paschal mystery for you? How do you celebrate that day? How does it enhance your paschal mystery spirituality?
4. How does paschal mystery spirituality foster wholeness in you?

---

22. Ibid.
23. Ibid.
24. Ibid.

Conclusion

BEGINNING WITH MY EXPERIENCE of dialogue with my friend about the death and new life occurring in our lives, I have led you on a spiritual journey. We began with an in-depth exploration of a phrase that appears frequently in *The Roman Missal*: paschal mystery. Understanding paschal mystery as the suffering, death, resurrection, ascension, and gift of the Spirit of Jesus, we noted how often the phrase or one of its cognate phrases appears in *The Roman Missal*. Then, we explored the biblical origin of the word *paschal* and *mystery*. In tracing this background, we noted how the death and resurrection of Jesus were reinterpreted by Christian Bible (New Testament) writers using the Hebrew Bible (Old Testament) image of the Passover lamb. By reflecting upon the paschal mystery of Jesus, we begin to see that what happened to Jesus is happening to us in our daily lives. The joining of Jesus' paschal mystery to an awareness of our paschal mystery is paschal mystery spirituality, a way of life.

While paschal mystery spirituality permeates *The Roman Missal*, it is especially presented during the Lent and Easter seasons and particularly present during the last week of Lent, known as Holy Week. Thus, we examined its presentation on Palm Sunday of the Passion of the Lord in general and specifically in each of the three-year cycle of gospel texts. We noted that suffering is understood as betrayal in Matthew's Gospel, that suffering is abandonment in Mark's Gospel, and that suffering is martyrdom in Luke's Gospel.

On Holy Thursday evening, The Sacred Paschal Triduum begins with the Lord's Supper, which not only recalls the paschal mystery of Jesus, but invites congregants to name where they find the five aspects of paschal mystery spirituality etched in their lives. The next day, Good Friday, is The Celebration of the Passion of the Lord. After a general introduction to the interpretative dynamics at play with the biblical texts for this celebration, we explored the paschal mystery in the Letter to the Hebrews, in John's Gospel, and in the adoration of the cross. Throughout the three sections on Good Friday, we looked at suffering and death from various biblical perspectives.

The Easter Vigil continues the focus on paschal mystery, especially in the biblical texts, and more specifically in the lives of those who are baptized during the vigil. They die and rise with Christ through the waters of baptism. They are given the gift of the Holy Spirit, and then they celebrate the paschal mystery that was just traced upon them in the Eucharist, itself the memorial of Jesus' paschal mystery. Because resurrection is on the other side of final death, we also explored the various metaphors employed by Christian Bible (New Testament) writers in their attempts to describe resurrected life.

Easter Sunday begins the fifty-day celebration of the Easter Season with its focus on paschal mystery spirituality. Both the prayers from *The Roman Missal* and the biblical texts focus on all five aspects of the paschal mystery. In this section, we explored further the gospel narratives concerning the resurrection to surface the various authors' understanding of resurrection. On the fortieth day of the Easter Season occurs the Ascension of the Lord, a unique Lukan story. Ascension is all about a new perspective. If we are living the changes we began during Lent, then by the time we get to the Ascension, our point of view should be altered.

The Easter Season finale is Pentecost Sunday, which marks the gift of the Spirit, the last aspect of the paschal mystery. In this section we traveled through the metaphors used to describe the Holy Spirit, especially those borrowed from theophanic events in the Hebrew Bible (Old Testament). In general the biblical texts invite us to create our own metaphors to describe the joining of our spirit to the Spirit.

In the last three chapters of this book, we traced the paschal mystery through the Anointing of the Sick; death, funerals, and Christian burial;

Conclusion

and several special celebrations occurring during the liturgical year. Our goal in traveling through the last three chapters was to understand how paschal mystery spirituality is traced throughout our lives from baptism to death. All throughout our lifetime journey, we discover that our suffering, death, resurrection, ascension, and gift of the Spirit are united to that of Jesus. What happened to him during his life happens to us during our life.

Through this work, my contention has been that the suffering, death, resurrection, ascension, and gift of the Spirit of Jesus form a universal theme that is traced in our lives. Living paschal mystery spirituality is not just understanding how it was lived by Jesus, but understanding how we live it today. Most of the conjunction is lost on modern people who are not engaged in the scholarly work of mining the links. Paschal mystery spirituality represents a rich seam of spiritual truth.

Thus, *Christ Our Passover Has Been Sacrificed* has presented Christ, God's anointed one, who suffered, died, rose, ascended, and sent the Holy Spirit to all who follow him as a model for paschal mystery spirituality. In a word, he passed over from death to new life. Thus, he is the new passover, replacing the lamb of the former one.

This book has been *A Guide through Paschal Mystery Spirituality*. All five aspects of the paschal mystery—suffering, death, resurrection, ascension, and gift of the Spirit of Jesus—have been explored in *The Roman Missal* and in the Bible. If Jesus' spirituality was characterized by those five aspects in his relationship with God, then ours must be characterized by the same. If Jesus was transformed through the aspects of his paschal mystery, then our transforming presence of an all-embracing God will occur through the same aspects.

My approach throughout this book has been from a mystical theological point of view, that is, through systematic reflection on the experience of a loving knowledge of God mediated through the prayers in *The Roman Missal*. I have explored paschal mystery spirituality in an attempt to appropriate the prayers of *The Roman Missal* and the biblical texts upon which the prayers are based in a systematic manner in an attempt to help the reader reflect upon it and connect his or her life experiences to it. At this point in the book, the reader, who has experienced God in ordinary daily living, is in the process of integrating those experiences of God by reflection using *The Roman Missal* and the Bible. Such awareness of paschal mystery spirituality now calls the reader to responsible living of it in ever-transformative relationships.

Bibliography

"Appendix 1: *Ordo Exsequiarum*, 1969, Introduction." In *Order of Christian Funerals*, 379–84. Totowa, NJ: Catholic Book, 1998.
"Appendix to the Order of Mass: Eucharistic Prayer for Reconciliation I." In *The Roman Missal: Study Edition*, 758–63. Collegeville, MN: Liturgical, 2012.
"Appendix to the Order of Mass: Eucharistic Prayer for Reconciliation II." In *The Roman Missal: Study Edition*, 766–771. Collegeville, MN: Liturgical, 2012.
"Appendix to the Order of Mass: Eucharistic Prayer for Use in Masses for Various Needs I." In *The Roman Missal: Study Edition*, 774–79. Collegeville, MN: Liturgical, 2012.
"Appendix to the Order of Mass: Eucharistic Prayer for Use in Masses for Various Needs II." In *The Roman Missal: Study Edition*, 780–85. Collegeville, MN: Liturgical, 2012.
"Appendix to the Order of Mass: Eucharistic Prayer for Use in Masses for Various Needs III." In *The Roman Missal: Study Edition*, 786–91. Collegeville, MN: Liturgical, 2012.
"Appendix to the Order of Mass: Eucharistic Prayer for Use in Masses for Various Needs IV." In *The Roman Missal: Study Edition*, 792–97. Collegeville, MN: Liturgical, 2012.
Boyer, Mark G. *Divine Presence: Elements of Biblical Theophanies*. Eugene, OR: Wipf and Stock, 2017.
———and Matthew S. Ver Miller. *Human Wholeness: A Spirituality of Relationship*. Eugene, OR: Wipf and Stock, 2015.
———. *Why Suffer? The Answer of Jesus*. Washington, DC: Pastoral, 1994.
Catechism of the Catholic Church. Washington, DC: United States Catholic Conference, 1994.
"Christian Initiation, General Introduction." In *Rite of Christian Initiation of Adults*, xiv–xviii. Washington, DC: United States Catholic Conference, 1988.

Bibliography

"Constitution on the Sacred Liturgy, The." In *Vatican Council II: The Conciliar and Post Conciliar Documents*, 1–36. Newport, NY: Costello, 1987.

"Easter Sunday of the Resurrection of the Lord: At the Mass during the Day." In *The Roman Missal: Study Edition*, 387–8. Collegeville, MN: Liturgical, 2012.

"Easter Sunday of the Resurrection of the Lord: The Easter Vigil in the Holy Night." In *The Roman Missal: Study Edition*, 343–86. Collegeville, MN: Liturgical, 2012.

Eucharistic Prayers for Masses with Children. Washington, DC: United States Conference of Catholic Bishops, 2011.

Feist, James. "Is God Real? A Linguistic View." *The Fourth R* 30:3 (2017) 11–13, 16, 24.

Finley, James. "Discovering Self in Discovering God." Center for Action and Contemplation. August 14, 2017. http://www.cac.org.

"Friday of the Passion of the Lord [Good Friday]." In *The Roman Missal: Study Edition*, 314–38. Collegeville, MN: Liturgical, 2012.

"General Introduction, Christian Initiation." In *Rite of Christian Initiation of Adults*, xiv–xviii. Washington, DC: United States Catholic Conference, 1988.

Hoffner, Erick. "As We Lay Dying: Stephen Jenkinson on How We Deny Our Mortality." *The Sun* August (2015) 4–13.

Jenkinson, Stephen. "As We Lay Dying: Stephen Jenkinson on How We Deny Our Mortality." Interview by Erik Hoffner. *The Sun* August (2015) 4–13.

Kramer, Kenneth Paul. *Martin Buber's Spirituality: Hasidic Wisdom for Everyday Life*. Lanham, MD: Rowman & Littlefield, 2013.

Lectionary for Mass. Volume I: Sundays, Solemnities, Feasts of the Lord, and the Saints. Totowa, NJ: Catholic Book, 1998.

Loades, Ann. "Mysticism: 'The Energetic Love' of a Female Adventurer." In *Exploring Lost Dimensions in Christian Mysticism: Opening to the Mystical*, edited by Louise Nelstrop and Simon D. Podmore, 117–29. Burlington, VT: Ashgate, 2013.

McCosker, Philip. "*Enhypostasia Mystica*: Contributions from Mystical Theology for a Tired Debate in Historical and Systematic Theology." In *Christian Mysticism and Incarnational Theology: Between Transcendence and Immanence*, edited by Louise Nelstrop and Simon D. Podmore, 69–92. Burlington, VT: Ashgate, 2013.

McKee, Tim. "The Geography of Sorrow: Francis Weller on Navigating Our Losses." *The Sun* October (2017) 4–13.

McKim, Donald K. *Westminster Dictionary of Theological Terms*. Louisville, KY: Westminster John Knox, 1996.

Migut, Boguslaw. "'The Study of the Liturgy:' The Origins and Current Significance of a Theological Discipline." *Worship* 91:5 (2017) 396–414.

Morgan, Ben. "How to Read a Mystical Text: Meister Eckhart Sermons 5a and 5b." In *Christian Mysticism and Incarnational Theology: Between Transcendence and Immanence*, edited by Louise Nelstrop and Simon D. Podmore, 93–106. Burlington, VT: Ashgate, 2013.

Nelstrop, Louise and Simon D. Podmore, eds. *Exploring Lost Dimensions in Christian Mysticism: Opening to the Mystical*. Burlington, VT: Ashgate, 2013.

———. *Christian Mysticism and Incarnational Theology: Between Transcendence and Immanence*. Burlington, VT: Ashgate, 2013.

O'Day, Gail R. and David Peterson, eds. *The Access Bible: New Revised Standard Version with the Apocryphal/Deuterocanonical Books*. New York, NY: Oxford University Press, 1999.

Order of Christian Funerals. Totowa, NJ: Catholic Book, 1998.

"Order of Mass, The." In *The Roman Missal: Study Edition*, 511–673. Collegeville, MN: Liturgical, 2012.

Osiek, Carolyn. "The Power of the Cross." *Worship* 91:3 (2017) 213–15.

"Palm Sunday of the Passion of the Lord." In *The Roman Missal: Study Edition*, 273–87. Collegeville, MN: Liturgical, 2012.

Pastoral Care of the Sick: Rites of Anointing and Viaticum. Collegeville, MN: Liturgical, 1983.

"Pentecost Sunday: At the Vigil Mass." In *The Roman Missal: Study Edition*, 445–52. Collegeville, MN: Liturgical, 2012.

Phiri, Felix Mabvuto. "Liturgical Participation and Apostolic Mission." *Worship* 91:3 (2017) 224–43.

Regan, Patrick. "The Centrality of the Paschal Mystery in the Missal of Paul VI." *Worship* 90:2 (2016) 126–38.

Rite of Christian Initiation of Adults. Washington, DC: United States Catholic Conference, 1988.

Rohr, Richard. "Dark Night of the Soul, The." Center for Action and Contemplation. September 7, 2017. http://www.cac.org.

———. "Human Development through Scripture." Center for Action and Contemplation. September 10, 2017. http://www.cac.org.

———. "Our Ultimate Identity." Center for Action and Contemplation. August 13, 2017. http://www.cac.org.

Roman Missal, The: Study Edition. Collegeville, MN: Liturgical, 2012.

Rothschild, Clare K. "Holy Sweat: Interpreting Luke's Portrait of Jesus in the Garden." *The Bible Today* 55:3 (2017) 186–92.

Seaman, Kristopher W. "How Does Baptism Change Us?" *Pastoral Liturgy* 48:3 (2017) insert between 16 and 17.

"Thursday of Holy Week [Holy Thursday]: The Chrism Mass." In *The Roman Missal: Study Edition*, 290–95. Collegeville, MN: Liturgical, 2012.

"Thursday of the Lord's Supper: At the Evening Mass." In *The Roman Missal: Study Edition*, 299–313. Collegeville, MN: Liturgical, 2012.

"Universal Norms on the Liturgical Year and the Calendar." In *The Roman Missal: Study Edition*, 110–35. Collegeville, MN: Liturgical, 2012.

Vatican Council II: The Conciliar and Post Conciliar Documents. Newport, NY: Costello, 1987.

Vinzent, Markus. "Neither Money nor Delights, but Daily Bread: The Extraordinary as Spiritual Temptation." In *Christian Mysticism and Incarnational Theology: Between Transcendence and Immanence*, edited by Louise Nelstrop and Simon D. Podmore, 107–130. Burlington, VT: Ashgate, 2013.

Welch, John. "Mystical Theology." In *The New Dictionary of Theology*, edited by Joseph A. Komonchak, Mary Collins, and Dermot A. Lane, 692–4. Wilmington, DE: Michael Glazier, 1987.

Weller, Francis. "The Geography of Sorrow: Francis Weller on Navigating Our Losses." Interview by Tim McKee. *The Sun* October (2017) 4–13.

White, David. "Liturgical Spirituality and the Rooted Heart." *Worship* 91:3 (2017) 244–50.

Zachhuber, Johannes. "Mysticism as a Social Type of Christianity? Ernst Troeltsch's Interpretation in its Historical and Systematic Context." In *Exploring Lost Dimensions in Christian Mysticism: Opening to the Mystical*, edited by Louise Nelstrop and Simon D. Podmore, 69–84. Burlington, VT: Ashgate, 2013.

Recent Books by Mark G. Boyer

Nature Spirituality: Praying with Wind, Water, Earth, Fire

A Spirituality of Ageing

Caroling through Advent and Christmas: Daily Reflections with Familiar Hymns

Weekday Saints: Reflections on Their Scriptures

Human Wholeness: A Spirituality of Relationship

The Liturgical Environment: What the Documents Say (third edition)

A Simple Systematic Mariology

Praying Your Way through Luke's Gospel and the Acts of the Apostles

Daybreaks: Daily Reflections for Advent and Christmas

Daybreaks: Daily Reflections for Lent and Easter

An Abecedarian of Animal Spirit Guides: Spiritual Growth through Reflections on Creatures

Overcome with Paschal Joy: Chanting through Lent and Easter—Daily Reflections with Familiar Hymns

Taking Leave of Your Home: Moving in the Peace of Christ

A Spirituality of Mission: Reflections for Holy Week and Easter

An Abecedarian of Sacred Trees: Spiritual Growth through Reflections on Woody Plants

Divine Presence: Elements of Biblical Theophanies

Fruit of the Vine: A Biblical Spirituality of Wine

Names for Jesus: Reflections for Advent and Christmas

Talk to God and Listen to the Casual Reply: Experiencing the Spirituality of John Denver

www.ingramcontent.com/pod-product-compliance
Lightning Source LLC
Chambersburg PA
CBHW071505150426
43191CB00009B/1420